TREATMENT

OR

TRANSFORMATION

13
REAL
STORIES
of why you can't
argue with a
changed life

NANCY ALCORN

Treatment or Transformation by Nancy Alcorn
Published by Mercy Multiplied
P.O. Box 111060
Nashville, TN 37222
www.MercyMultiplied.com

Scripture references may be taken from one of the following versions of the
Holy Bible:

New King James Version of the Bible, Copyright © 1979, 1980, 1982 by
Thomas Nelson, Inc., publishers. Used by permission.

New Living Translation, copyright © 1996, 2004, 2007, 2013, 2015 by Tyndale
House Foundation. Used by permission of Tyndale House Publishers Inc.,
Carol Stream, Illinois 60188. All rights reserved.

New International Version® NIV® Copyright © 1973, 1978, 1984 by International
Bible Society® Used by permission. All rights reserved worldwide.

Cover Design by Jay Smith at Juicebox Designs www.juiceboxdesigns.com

Typesetting by Mandi Cofer at The Tiny Typesetter www.thetinytypesetter.com

Visit the Author's Page at www.MercyMultiplied.com

International Standard Book Number: 978-0-9986485-3-8

First Edition
Printed in the USA

Dedication

To Jesus Christ, the One and Only One,
who can transform and heal a life that is
so broken. A special thanks to these thirteen
courageous women who represent the
thousands of young women who have either
received help through Mercy Multiplied
or walked through the doors of a
Mercy home over the last 35 years.

About the Author

Nancy Alcorn spent the first eight years of her career working for the state of Tennessee. Her time with the government included five years with the Department of Corrections working with the juvenile delinquent girls, and three years with the Department of Human Services working in Emergency Protective Services investigating child abuse cases and supervising foster care.

It was during this time of government work that Nancy realized the inadequacy of these programs to offer real transformation in the lives of troubled individuals. Out of this experience came a driving passion for broken young girls that led to the birth of Mercy in 1983. Today, Mercy Multiplied serves young women in locations across the nation and around the world and reaches thousands through its outreach resources and events. People have come from all over the world to study Mercy's successful program model in faith based residential care.

An accomplished author and passionate speaker, Nancy

travels extensively, sharing the mission and work of Mercy Multiplied and empowering audiences with practical principles to walk in life-long freedom. Nancy resides in Nashville, TN, the home of Mercy Multiplied's national headquarters.

About Mercy Multiplied

Mercy Multiplied is a nonprofit Christian organization dedicated to helping young women break free from life-controlling behaviors and situations, including eating disorders, self-harm, drug and alcohol addictions, unplanned pregnancy, depression, sexual abuse, and sex trafficking. We hope to help every person we serve experience God's unconditional love, forgiveness, and life-transforming power.

Mercy's residential program is voluntary, biblically based, and completely free of charge to young women ages 13-28. It uses proven methods and counselors, lasts approximately six to nine months, and features a multi-dimensional approach to heal spirit, soul, and body. We address the root causes of the issues women face, rather than merely medicating symptoms or modifying external behavior. Our goal is to help residents permanently stop destructive cycles, discover purpose for their lives, and become productive and thriving individuals.

Founded by Nancy Alcorn in 1983, the first Mercy home

was opened in Monroe, LA. Today Mercy homes exist in Monroe, LA; Nashville, TN; Sacramento, CA; and St. Louis, MO. International affiliates exist in the United Kingdom, Canada, and New Zealand. Our homes are specifically designed to be a place where residents feel safe and cared for in a home environment.

Mercy Multiplied is committed to expanding outreach initiatives and to "multiplying" Mercy outside of our residential homes for both men and women. Our outreach activities are designed to educate leaders, equip individuals, and empower churches. Our programs and resources are based on the same biblically based, life-transforming principles used by Mercy homes for over 35 years in helping troubled young women find lasting freedom and live an empowered Christian life.

For more information, please visit
www.MercyMultiplied.com

Contents

Acknowledgements

No project like this is ever possible alone, and I have been blessed with an awesome team of people who caused all of the elements of this book to come together. I want to extend my personal thanks to the following:

Joel Kilpatrick—for the countless hours you spent writing, editing and providing input on this project. Without your belief in our mission and your help in gathering the details of these 13 stories, this book would not have been possible.

Melanie Wise—for your tireless help in writing, editing, and providing invaluable input on this book

Tyra Woodall, Sarah Vaughn, and the entire Transitional Care Team—for investing in every graduate and former resident, specifically the 13 who are represented in this book

Leah Hayes, Rachel Bedenbaugh, Natalie Moore, and the entire Marketing Team—for your creative ideas, suggestions, and many hours of work to create such an excellent book and corresponding videos

Dr. Brooke Keels, Jamillah Jackson, Rebecca Manning, Kelly Lane and Andrea Martinez—for your expertise in reading, editing, and making suggestions while continuing your workload at Mercy

A special thanks to our partners who continually give financially to make it possible for innumerable people to experience healing and freedom.

Last, but not least, to the amazing Board members and staff at Mercy who are God's special gift to me and to this ministry. You are the very best!

Introduction

For the first eight years of my career, I worked for the state of Tennessee at a correctional facility for juvenile delinquent females and investigated child abuse cases. While serving in these positions, I came across programs that, unfortunately, were not producing permanent results. What was being offered as an "answer" to those hurting young women was not changing their lives for the better. Tragically, some of them committed suicide before their 18th birthdays, and others were killed in street gang fights or died from drug overdoses. Others continued in the prison system or remained in the cycle of abuse they had come to know as a normal way of life. Through this process, God revealed to me that treatment wasn't enough; He desired their lives to be totally transformed.

Most of the young women who reach out to Mercy Multiplied for help have gone through a treatment program of some type, whether it be an addiction, eating disorder, or psychiatric program. It is not uncommon for a Mercy applicant to have gone through *multiple* treatment programs. I recognize the value that these programs add in supporting and stabilizing people, and I understand that there is a time and place for this type of treatment.

In fact, since Mercy is not a medical facility, it is sometimes necessary to refer young women to other treatment programs before entering our program. For example, if a young woman struggling with an eating disorder applies but is not at a medically safe weight, we will refer her to a treatment program to become medically stable prior to entering Mercy. Or if a young woman is struggling with a severe drug addiction, we will refer her to a treatment facility so that she is able to safely detox from the substances before entering one of our homes.

Unfortunately, as I have seen during my time at Mercy since 1983, the history of the young women we work with show that many of them have been in treatment programs where they have been labeled and told that they can never live a normal life. They are told that they will always struggle with their issues. We know this is not true. There is a step beyond treatment; it is *transformation*.

People often focus their attention only on what they can see. They work hard to "fix" themselves by concentrating on their unwanted behaviors. They address their hurts from the outside-in, with the hope that once the unwanted behavior is gone, they will be healthy. However, simply correcting negative behaviors does not produce a real heart change. We see this when young women relapse, or even trade one addiction for another, because they have not addressed the root issues underneath their behaviors. They are simply shuffling bondage around. Behavior modification does not bring healing and freedom and transformation from the inside-out.

Only Jesus can do that! We have to get to the root causes of our issues if we really want to live free and stay free!

I am about to share 13 different stories that will provide you with **13 REAL STORIES of why you can't argue with a changed life.** These stories contain powerful examples of how God intervened and brought complete transformation. The young women you will read about in the coming pages represent thousands upon thousands of girls who have received the same transformation since 1983 at Mercy's multiple locations existing in the U.S.A. and other nations.

Through Mercy's Outreach Program, men and women of all ages are learning about the principles of freedom that I wrote about in my last book, *Ditch the Baggage* and our new study, *Keys to Freedom*. We receive testimonies on a regular basis from people all over the world who are experiencing new levels of freedom in their lives, because they have invited the Holy Spirit to expose the root causes of their struggles and to transform them from the inside-out.

I am on a mission for faith to be built up in the heart of anyone who reads this book. There is no such thing as a life that cannot be transformed when someone allows God to work in their heart and life. I want you to know that, through the power of Christ, you can overcome whatever issues or hurts you may be struggling with. You do not have to live your life under a list of labels or diagnoses. You do not have to stay in bondage to all of the things you have experienced. In fact, those are the very things that God will restore and use to be a part of your testimony of freedom. My hope and prayer is that the following 13 stories will encourage you to believe for greater levels of freedom in your own life and

AUTHOR'S NOTE

In early 2017, I began hearing about a new Netflix series called *13 Reasons Why*, and a friend of mine, who is familiar with the issues we deal with at Mercy, encouraged me to watch the first season. I was deeply impacted by this series, as I quickly realized how many young women who walk through the doors of our residential homes have similar struggles as the girl featured in the series. I was inspired to share 13 stories of young women who experienced a very different outcome than the girl featured in *13 Reasons Why* because they chose to reach out for help.

reason
ONE

Porsha

One day when Porsha was three years old, she and her mother were walking down the sidewalk a few blocks from her grandmother's house. A van pulled up. Porsha's mom sat Porsha down on a nearby rock.

"You stay here," she said. "I'm going to be right back." With that, she headed for the van.

"Who's that?" the driver asked, gesturing at Porsha.

"A neighborhood kid," Porsha's mom said. Sometimes her mom called Porsha "my niece," but never "my daughter"—at least not to the people who came to pick her mom up.

The van pulled away and Porsha sat on the rock. An hour went by. Two hours. Three hours. Five hours. It started to get dark.

I don't think she's coming back, Porsha thought, and hopped off the rock. Her stomach growled as she walked in the direction of her grandmother's house. Bursting in the door she announced, "Grandma, I'm hungry!"

Her grandmother came in to see who it was.

"Porsha, where's your mom?" she asked, looking behind her and seeing no one.

"I don't know," Porsha answered.

"Where have you been?" Grandma asked.

"Sitting on a rock."

"A rock where?"

"Out by the street. Mom left in a van."

A pause.

"For how long?"

"All day," Porsha said as if it were common, which it was.

Her grandmother looked at her with astonishment.

"Porsha, you don't have a fear radar," she said, taking her granddaughter by the hand and leading her into the kitchen.

"Next time that happens, you run right over here. There are real dangers out there."

For Porsha, it was just another day as the child of someone who had been addicted to crack since before her birth. Porsha was born premature, weighing just three pounds. By God's grace, there was nothing wrong with Porsha physically, but she came into a fractured family: a father jailed for grand theft auto and addicted to heroin; a mother who used drugs and bounced from house to house, essentially homeless, with Porsha in tow.

The state eventually intervened and Porsha was put into foster care with a younger brother she didn't know she had. Her mother had left him at the hospital upon his birth, and the state put them together.

"Cool! I have a little brother," Porsha exclaimed when introduced to him, and took on the protective role of an older sister. Their foster mother had two kids of her own. Everything was nice for a while. Porsha went to preschool. Life was stable. Then the woman seemed to single Porsha out for extra discipline and bizarre punishments: food deprivation, "whoopings," even forcing her to stay up all night standing in the corner.

"If I find you asleep, I'll beat you," the foster mother promised, and so Porsha would stand all night in fear, her legs going numb. The next day she kept falling down the stairs because her legs were so stiff. As a result, she feared staircases.

One night a female teenage babysitter watched Porsha alone at home. The girl sexually abused Porsha, introducing a new level of pain and confusion into her five-year-old mind.

What the heck just happened? Porsha wondered.

Around the same time, she began waking up to find men in her bed.

One morning Porsha woke up next to a man and went to tell her foster mother. "Just go back to sleep and by the time you wake up, they will be gone," her foster mother told her. She was right. Porsha fell asleep and woke up alone—but deeply confused.

While visiting family one time, with her foster mother in the room, Porsha blurted out, "People come visit me and I have men in my bed."

Family members looked at each other with alarm.

Back at home, her foster mother called her to the basement.

"You shouldn't lie about men being in your bed," she warned. "If you say that again, you know what will happen."

Porsha knew: whoopings, isolation, strange and brutal discipline. Her foster mother only skipped punishments when a county worker was scheduled to visit soon. She always treated Porsha nicer and fed her more before the visits.

One day I'm going to get out of here, Porsha told herself when the whoopings returned. *One day I'm going to get adopted.*

She didn't actually know what "adopted" meant, but to her, it meant not having to live in that foster home anymore.

The dream finally materialized right before her sixth birthday. Porsha's grandmother on her father's side took her out of foster care and into her home, while her younger brother went to live with an aunt. Porsha couldn't run fast enough out of the house which had become to her a chamber of horrors.

"I don't know how she's going to deal with you," her foster mother called out to Porsha by way of good-bye, then slammed the front door shut.

I don't care what you say, Porsha thought. *I don't have to be there anymore!*

Her family threw a "welcome home" party for her, but when real life resumed, Porsha was left home alone most of the day. Both grandparents worked long hours—Granny for a university hospital, her grandfather for the city. Both came home tired each night, plodded through their nightly routines and headed to sleep. Porsha did everything she could to gain her Granny's acceptance—cooking dinner, cleaning the house, dusting the blinds—but it never seemed to be enough.

One day, older boy relatives came to the house while Porsha was alone. She thought they wanted to play. Instead, they began sexually abusing her. She was seven.

Here we go again, Porsha thought. *I can't tell Granny— she's already sick and sad that my mom is on drugs. More bad news will make her sicker, or my mom will find out and over-dose like Granny worries about.*

So the abuse continued for years. When Porsha was alone, she filled a journal with her thoughts.

Someone deprived me of my life, she wrote one day as she got older. *I feel invisible even at school. No one notices me. The teacher marks me absent when I'm sitting in class. So I guess I am invisible.*

She took on that persona, stopping schoolwork and retreating into herself. Some nights she looked in the mirror and ripped out her hair, or scratched herself with her finger-nails until she bled, because she had become so numb.

I want to feel something, she thought. *I feel nothing.*

The first suicide attempt happened at age nine. She filled a two-liter bottle with bleach, cough syrup, cleaning supplies, Tylenol and whatever else she could find. It didn't seem to do any harm. Her stomach burned, but life went on.

That should have killed me, but I'm not dead, Porsha thought.

She tried again with various methods—seven times. Nothing worked.

I can't die, she concluded. *I must be indestructible. People beat me and I don't die. They starve me and I don't die. They rape me and I don't die. I must be some kind of superhero.*

As the abuse continued and Porsha turned ten, she became virtually mute. People greeted her and she just stared at them. The school finally called her grandmother.

"Porsha is not responding to anything," they said. "She won't talk to us."

Counselors appeared, all saying the same things, sitting across the table from her.

"Not talking is not helping. What's wrong?" they asked.

"I'm hurting," Porsha would reply.

"What's hurting you?" they asked.

How do I explain that I am being sexually abused by several relatives every day after school?

Porsha shrugged. "I can't explain," she said.

"But you have to," the counselors pressed.

I don't think you can handle what has happened to me, Porsha concluded. And so she clammed up again.

But when Porsha was 12 years old, she met with a counselor who was young and seemed well-meaning.

"Just tell me your story," she invited.

Porsha thought a moment.

"Do you really want to know?" she asked.

"Yes, I want to know," the counselor replied hopefully. Porsha felt an almost volcanic rage rise within her. She slapped both hands on the table.

"Do you really want to know?" she asked louder.

"I really want to know," the counselor said with a brave face.

Porsha launched into her story—what had happened in foster care, the men in her bed, the abuse by relatives, the neglect by her mother and others.

"So, do you care now?" she ended. The counselor, baffled, jaw open, reached to pick up the phone but kept fumbling it. When she had summoned someone on the other end of the line, she did something no other counselor had done: got up, walked around the desk and embraced Porsha.

Is she going to violate me, too? Porsha wondered at first. Then Porsha felt emotions inside of her own heart—real emotions, accompanied by real tears. She marveled at the experience.

This feels like good touch, she thought. *This feels safe and kind. I will never forget this hug.*

She went to the hospital and spent several days in the company of doctors and nurses.

"I don't want to be here," she told them.

"You need medication," they said.

"I don't want to be on medication. I just told the lady I got sexually abused and beaten. I'm hurting and I just want the pain to be gone," Porsha said.

"Yes, but you need medication so you can go back to school," they said.

I'm suffering on a whole other level, and nobody's paying attention, she wanted to reply.

Then came their attempted diagnoses: bipolar, schizophrenic—"crazy," in Porsha's words.

They're all trying to figure out my psychosis, but I'm not crazy, she thought. *But if they want crazy, I'll give them crazy.*

Back at school, and on anti-depressant medications, Porsha became the out-of-control person they labeled her to be.

I'll show them bipolar and schizophrenic, she thought while shoving around a classmate, exploring a newfound aggression.

The young, kind counselor was gone and every counseling session now seemed the same.

"Are you taking your medications?"

"Yes," Porsha answered.

"Are you going to your groups?"

"Yes."

"How are you feeling?"

"I'm not feeling anything."

"Maybe we should adjust your medications."

Porsha's abusers had been investigated but not punished. She was no longer left alone for them to prey on, but her years of pain remained.

I still remember what happened to me, and I want to explore that, she thought. *But apparently nobody wants to hear about it. They just want to teach me "coping skills" and give me pills to numb me.*

In her early teens, Porsha weaned herself off all medications—and grew into her self-designated role as the school's bully. She particularly targeted kids who got bullied by others. Her goal was to teach them to stand up for themselves.

"You can't let people take advantage of you," she said while pushing them around. "You're just gonna let me smack you in the face and do all this stuff to you? Your self-esteem is that low?"

When they stood up to her, she left them alone as a reward.

Soon she was controlling every kid on her block with

intimidation and beatings. "I am nobody to be messed with" was her creed, and everybody lived under the shadow of her rage.

One day when Porsha was 15 years old, she was in her room drawing and writing, overcome with frustration at the state of her life. She had always believed there was a God but had never talked to Him before. She filled pages with her feelings and said to Him, "If You like me, You had better talk back to me right now."

She pointed to her bed and announced, "I got abused in this bed. But nobody cares or wants to hear about it. I've been neglected in this home, but they make me stay here. They call me crazy, and maybe they're right because I feel like I'm losing my mind right now."

She paused, then continued, "But I don't need that. I need peace of mind. I need You to talk to me."

Suddenly, a warm blanket of peace descended on her. It wrapped her up like a big hug. Porsha wept.

"Go to the bathroom," a voice inside said. It seemed trustworthy and kind, so she went and stared at herself in the mirror. It was like seeing herself for the first time. God's voice came—she knew it was His now.

I love you. You belong to Me. You're My child.

Thoughts of suicide fled far away, like they had never existed.

I belong to somebody, Porsha affirmed. *I am loved. He wants me, and I'm going to fight for this love if it's the last thing I do.*

Her aggression continued, but now it wasn't self-destructive—it was a way of fighting for her life.

At 17, Porsha went to live with a cousin in Toledo, finished high school and became involved in a church. They welcomed and encouraged her so much that her heart began to repair. But something was missing, and she found herself in spells of depression. If she made any small mistake, she desperately hid it because she thought somebody would yell at her. Only perfection could keep her safe, she thought.

At one point, the depression went so deep that she tried suicide one last time and landed in a psychiatric unit. When she got out, her mentor at the church picked her up and said, "I have a surprise for you." She took her to a restaurant where her church family and pastors had gathered to celebrate her life.

They're not even making me feel crazy, Porsha thought. *They're having normal conversations with me. Y'all know I just tried to kill myself?!*

The display of love so moved her that she wept publicly for the first time in her life.

She also agreed, at her pastor's recommendation, to apply to Mercy Multiplied. The day she was accepted, she ran into the church office.

"I got accepted to Mercy!" she announced. Everybody stopped what they were doing to gather around and cheer. At her going-away party they presented letters and personal notes, including children's drawings. She opened a new one every hour on the drive to Louisiana.

Porsha embraced everything God had for her at Mercy—the classes, the other girls, the daily schedule, the Bible study. She even wrote original worship songs and became the "head kitchen prep", which meant preparing food, keeping inventory, pulling out snacks—and getting her crew up an hour early to make breakfast, not always an easy task.

Porsha especially loved her bed because it was the first one where she had not been violated.

Hearing about the value of forgiveness, she longed to reconcile with her parents somehow.

I want a relationship with my dad and mom but I don't know how because they're like strangers to me, she wrote in her journal. *I don't know how to get close to them.*

Porsha's father had gotten out of jail and made a decision to leave his past behind, get a job, go to church and get an education. The stability in his life made it possible for he and Porsha to be reconciled. Her dad finished college, got a good job in the technology industry, and was financially stable.

Restoring relationship with her mother was more difficult. Porsha held onto blame for the way her mother had neglected her, which had led to so many painful experiences at the hands of others. But Porsha believed God's Word: forgiveness is the only way out of the prison of pain.

God, help me to have a mother again, she prayed. *I forgive her by faith for everything that happened to me. Help me to love and accept her. Help us to have a relationship someday.*

While at Mercy, Porsha also began to dream again—literal dreams in the night which carried meaning or direction for her or a friend. She'd had such dreams from a young age, but now they came back with clarity.

One night she dreamt she was graduating from Mercy on a certain date with three other girls.

They've been here longer than me, Porsha thought, laughing when she woke up. *There's no way I'm graduating with them!*

But it happened just as she had dreamt. She was given that graduation date. Her mentors from the church came down, and her pastor video-conferenced in for the big day in October of 2013.

"I call this my love story, because that's what God gave me: love," Porsha said, introducing her testimony that day. "Love is what I didn't understand and what was lacking. Now love, encouragement and peace of mind are my most powerful gifts. The enemy tried to shut me up, but he didn't win. God wins! His love is more powerful than anything."

While at Mercy, Porsha learned a variety of life skills, including how to interview for a job, what to wear and how to conduct herself at work. She also learned personal finances and budgeting through Dave Ramsey's Financial Peace University program. Back in Ohio, Porsha had a strong support group at the church that helped her set up a game plan for how to utilize the things she had learned for successful living.

It wasn't long until she got a job working with girls who had been through the same kinds of experiences she went through. Using much of what she learned at Mercy Multiplied, she taught them daily routines to get their lives back on track. But she did more: she loved them and listened to their stories. When they gave her trouble or acted out, she told them, "I'm gonna stand here and love you because that's what God did for me."

Doors also opened to create new relationships with her parents. She and her father had been talking more, and for Thanksgiving in 2015, Porsha traveled to his home and cooked for the family. The conversation was deeply meaningful, especially when her father expressed his great pride in her.

Not long after her visit with her Father, Porsha began talking with her mom. Conversations were awkward at first. Indeed, it was a miracle to Porsha that they were speaking at all, but her mother's new husband insisted they bridge the gap. He had been a God-send to their family, walking Porsha's mother through drug rehabilitation and getting them plugged into a church in Florida where they lived.

In 2015, Porsha's church prepared for its annual celebration honoring people who were involved in leading worship and Sunday services. Each year, awards were given out, appreciation was shown and everyone had a good time. Each year, it seemed like everybody's families attended and celebrated with them—except for Porsha's.

You know what? This year I'm going to invite my mom, Porsha told herself, stirring up her courage.

And she made the call.

"Mom?" Porsha said, gulping down any remaining fear. "We're having this event at church, and I know you live far away, but I'd really like you to come."

"Oh, I would love to," her mother replied.

The pair spent a three-day weekend shopping, staying in a hotel and catching up on healing conversations that had never happened.

"With everything I was going through, I didn't know if you'd make it, Porsha," her mother told her through tears, "but here you are working, graduated from high school without me, and doing all these amazing things. I hope when I grow up, I'm more like you!"

At the church celebration, everyone erupted with joy when they saw Porsha arrive.

"Your mom's here!" they exclaimed, and hugged them both.

During a raffle drawing at the event, Porsha leaned over to her mother.

"We're going to win! I just know it," she whispered.

The ticket number was called and Porsha and her mother won a five-day cruise. Everyone applauded, and for Porsha, it was about more than winning a prize—it was a celebration of a relationship that had come back from the dead.

"I just love the glow on your face and the confidence," her mother said as she departed. "It's such a beautiful thing, what your life has become."

Porsha currently maintains deep spiritual roots. She spends many hours with God, cherishing His presence and knowing that He enjoys spending time with her as Father and daughter. At church she helps lead worship, and sometimes comes to the sanctuary alone during the week to spend time in prayer. When depression or heaviness tries to return, she anchors to a deeper joy, exercises her authority as a follower of Christ and speaks truth against those lies, just as she learned at the Mercy home.

Porsha continues to work as a house leader at a group home for people with various disabilities. She pours out love on them from the overflow of love God has given her. She also has found financial stability for the first time in her life and is pressing into all that God has ahead for her.

Her mother's husband, the man who had been such a God-send in her life, suddenly passed away in 2016. It was a tough time for her mother, but Porsha was there for her and the two of them now live together. Porsha has received more and more opportunities to share her story publicly and advocate for hurting people. By nature an encourager, she is writing a book to give people tools for maintaining freedom and walking successfully through everyday life. Her goal is to graduate from college with a degree in communications.

"When I tell my story I feel like I'm describing a different person," Porsha said recently. "Everything about me has changed. My heart was broken at one point, but God created it to love and to be loved. That's the life I have now."

———————

Porsha's story of transformation never ceases to amaze me. The levels of abuse that she suffered at the hands of so many people is just excruciating. The neglect and abandonment that she experienced from her parents—the ones who should have cared for and nurtured Porsha—is difficult to even comprehend. As a young child, Porsha should have been living a safe and carefree life. Instead, she was tossed around from family to family, desperate for love and security.

It breaks my heart to think of the pain that Porsha experienced as a child, but that's why the power of forgiveness in her story is so amazing. She suffered neglect, betrayal, abuse, and disappointment. And while Porsha's response to these hurts as a teen was anger and defensiveness, Porsha learned about the power of forgiveness at Mercy. She learned that choosing not to forgive those who had hurt her would be choosing to allow the process of bitterness and resentment to slowly kill her from the inside out.

The fact is that life can be harsh. We will all inevitably suffer some degree of hurt and pain along the way. But the level of damage we sustain is not dependent on the severity of the offense; it's dependent on our *response* to it. We may not be able to choose what happens to us, but we can choose how we will respond. If we choose to forgive, we choose life and freedom!

Forgiveness is part of God's heart towards us. It's in His nature to forgive, and His desire, in fact, His *commandment*, is that we also forgive. Colossians 3:13 says, "Bear with each other and forgive one another if any of you has a grievance against someone. Forgive as the Lord forgave you." God's commandment to forgive is not because He wants to make our lives difficult, but because He knows that forgiveness is a significant key to our walking in freedom.

I have heard many people say, "I can't forgive until the person who hurt me apologizes." It can be so difficult to forgive people when they show no remorse and seem to have moved on with their lives. However, whether the other person has asked for forgiveness or not, forgiving someone is an act of obedience. Forgiveness is not an emotional decision and may not even feel fair. If Porsha had waited for an apology from her mother, father, or foster mom to forgive, she may have waited forever. In the meantime, Porsha's life would have been the one affected by unforgiveness, not those who had hurt her.

Forgiveness is not a feeling, but it is a decision. It is an act of obedience. As you make the choice to forgive, your feelings may be pulling you in the opposite direction, but you have the opportunity to choose obedience over your emotions. You ultimately make the decision to forgive by *faith,* and as you continually make this choice, the feelings will follow the choice, and your heart will no longer be stuck in the hurt.

For Porsha, forgiveness was the start of reconciliation with her parents, but there are times when reconciling is not possible. While forgiveness is not earned, *trust is.* We are not expected to blindly trust someone who has hurt us. If the other person is unrepentant, unchanging, or unsafe for you, it is not necessary to seek reconciliation. You can still release forgiveness towards those who have hurt you while also putting up healthy boundaries in your life with unsafe people. In Porsha's story, we see that there had been true heart change in her mother and father, so Porsha was able to reconcile with them and allow them back into her life.

I love how Porsha was so intentional about connecting with a church community after she graduated from Mercy. One of the things that we work on with the residents in the Mercy program is their "Aftercare Plan". We help to connect them with a church in the area where they will live, as well as an accountability partner that they meet with on a weekly basis after they graduate. The community that Porsha was part of after her graduation was vitally important in supporting her and helping her to walk out all that she had learned at Mercy.

Psalm 92:13 says that we "flourish" when we choose to be "planted in the house of the Lord," which is His church, His people, and His body. God's heart is that each of us connect to a community of believers who will pray for us, support us, encourage us, and offer accountability. The Church is our spiritual family. And while no church is perfect, and no group of people is without fault, having a family of believers around you is an important part of walking in freedom, just as it was for Porsha.

Porsha graduated from our Louisiana home in 2013, and over two years later, at the end of 2015, we invited Porsha to be our featured graduate testimony at a live Evening of Mercy event, which included a sit-down dinner with over 700 people. This was truly one of my most amazing memories of Porsha. I had the privilege of introducing her to our guests that evening, and I will never forget how she came to the microphone with such great poise and confidence. She brought the house down with her story. Porsha spoke directly from her heart, and the crowd was so moved by the power of both her words and her story, in amazement at all she had overcome. This once broken young woman exuded such confidence and such a gift of communication and speaking that she is still using to this day. No one can deny how the power of Christ has radically transformed Porsha's life!

reason
TWO

Heather

The youngest of three children, Heather was, by her father's description, their most joyful child—free-spirited, humorous, and highly social. She grew up in a stable, peaceful Christian household in suburban Nashville where kids played in the cul de sac and a creek ran in the nearby woods. Heather was tall—almost six feet. When harsh remarks about her weight in middle school caused her to jump into sports, she found a fun, competitive community and a popularity she had never enjoyed before. Because of her active social life, her parents found that they needed to create curfews and limitations for her that they hadn't needed with their other children.

Heather didn't like the limitations her parents placed on her, so she began restricting eating as a quiet protest to "punish" them. Eating less also kept her thin and popular at school, which she enjoyed. Because their family ate together, attended church together, and her mother was a stay-at-home mom, Heather couldn't restrict her diet too much. But she controlled what she could. She began drinking at parties in high school, yet her mom, who seemed to have a hotline directly to God, always found out.

College gave her a ticket to freedom. Heather joined the volleyball team, and when drinking led to her dismissal from the team—a humiliating moment—she joined the track team which had looser rules. By the end of freshman year she had good grades and was popular on campus, but was drinking several days a week.

Things changed that summer. Back home, Heather attended a party at a friend's house down the street—a high school reunion of sorts. Then Heather struck up a conversation with a guy she knew from high school.

"Heather," he said, "let's forget about high school. You're a new person. Let me make you a drink."

She accepted, and that was the last thing she remembered. The drink had been drugged, and another guy she had never met led her to an upstairs bedroom. At some point, a male friend of Heather's wondered where she had gone. "They're upstairs dancing," someone said. The friend searched and found the guy assaulting her in a bed. Rushing in, he tore him off of Heather and slammed him against the wall, leaving a hole. Heather vaguely remembered the altercation and the brief ride home, where her friends sneaked her into her room.

She knew she had been raped.

I wasn't supposed to be there, she thought the next day. *This is my fault. This is why my parents said not to go to parties like that. I can't ever tell them what happened.*

A few days later, she headed back to college in East Tennessee, and life spun out of control. Her self-image plummeted, and she began to see herself as trash, easily manipulated—a piece of imitation artwork that was continually being marked down. Distrust pervaded relationships, and alcohol became her numbing agent. She also quit eating, purposely becoming skinny and unhealthy as a passive way of blaming the world for her pain: *Look at what happened to me. I got hurt, and this is what I have become.* At the same time, she was consumed with guilt over the rape.

Now and then, a friend would call her parents when Heather seemed to have gone too far, and her mother would bring her home for the weekend, several hours away from the college she attended near Knoxville, Tennessee. But the changes made at home were never permanent. Back at college, she would return to the same lifestyle, even while making the dean's list every semester, primarily as a way of deceiving her parents into thinking everything was okay.

I just want the pain to end, she thought many times. *This is slow suicide. I'm not brave enough to do it quickly, but it'll end the same way.*

To gain a sense of control in relationships, she became promiscuous, sometimes dating several guys at one time and allowing the relationships to be physical but never emotionally deep. She liked the feeling of power it gave her. *I wasn't in control that night,* she thought, *but I am now.* Whenever someone wanted to get to know her better, she cut him off and moved on to the next guy.

More than once she felt the tug of the Holy Spirit, and His whisper, *Heather, this is not you.* Now and then, in what seemed like out-of-body experiences, she observed what she was doing and thought, *This isn't what you do! This isn't Heather. You're made to be somebody else.*

But pain locked her into a cycle of damaging behavior. College ended and friends eased into careers and families. But Heather's lifestyle didn't change. In fact, it grew worse.

She stayed in Knoxville and threw herself into her career as a middle school teacher, working 12-hour days, then going to bars. She drank herself to unconsciousness every night and fueled her days with caffeine and barely any food. Some mornings, she woke up and didn't remember how she had gotten home. Or she noticed scrapes on the side of her car because apparently she had run off the road.

Serial, shallow relationships with men continued, along with Heather's habit of rejecting any guy who showed interest beyond the physical.

I'm not getting hurt again, Heather promised herself. *I'd rather hurt them first.*

Now and then, she attended church, trying to start afresh. Her parents, sensing their daughter's isolation and pain, urged her to see a counselor, to eat more, and to move closer to home. For years, they both labored in prayer for Heather, begging God to intervene, sometimes for hours a day. But apart from a few counseling sessions, shame over her lifestyle kept Heather in hiding.

They can't know what happened, or how I live now, she thought. *It would break their hearts.*

Prayer brought her parents to a point of iron resolve: *We are unable to help her now—but God can. We have to trust Him with her life. Our power comes from crying out to Him, and never stopping until we receive the answer.*

For years, Heather had used running as a requirement for eating, keeping a meticulous count of the calories she expended and seeing food as a reward for exercise. If she didn't exercise, she didn't eat. Now, craving a greater sense of control, she incorporated binging and purging. She was soon down to 100 pounds, unable to exercise anymore and suffering increasing health problems.

This isn't over, the Holy Spirit's voice came many nights. *This is not how it's going to end for you.*

But, Lord, my dysfunction feels so normal that anything healthy seems abnormal to me, she answered. *It's like being in a pit: the mud starts to feel nice and cool and comforting. But I'm shutting everyone out who cares for me. I know this isn't Your plan.*

One Easter, while sitting at home with her mom, Heather burst into tears.

"Mom, I'm not okay," she said. "I need help and don't know how to ask for it."

After comforting her and letting her cry for a while, her mother finally spoke.

"Do you remember that wedding we went to, where we met the girl who went to a Mercy home?" she asked.

Heather did remember sitting at a table with a young lady who was attending Mercy Multiplied. At the time Heather had thought, *That's good for you,* but hadn't made a connection with her own life.

"What's that got to do with me?" Heather replied.

"What if you did that?" her mom suggested.

"Mom, I'm a grown woman with a job. I can't take six months off of my life!" Heather exclaimed. "And how would I afford it? I've been to counselors and therapy. They cost a lot and none of it has worked."

"Heather," her mother asked pointedly, "if you don't, what life will you have?"

That night, Heather looked at Mercy Multiplied's website, read testimonies, watched videos, and was shocked to learn that the program was free of charge. The next afternoon, she was surprised to see family members and friends arriving at the house even though her mom wasn't cooking anything for dinner.

This is weird, Heather thought. *Why are they all here?*

Then she realized, *This is an intervention!*

Tempted to bolt from the house, Heather was too weak to run. And anyway, her brother was guarding the nearest door. Her community gathered around her, and for the next few hours poured out their hearts of love and concern as Heather listened and wept.

I need this, she thought. *I actually want this to happen.*

When her grandmother spoke about a son she had lost to bulimia, drug addiction and alcoholism, it nearly broke Heather's heart.

"When I look at the road you're on," her grandmother said, "it reminds me of your uncle."

Oh, my gosh, this is serious, Heather thought. *That's how my life will end if I continue like this.*

Hugging everyone, she went immediately upstairs, printed out the Mercy Multiplied application and sent it in. She was accepted and invited to the California home. By the time she flew out, she was weak and frail, yet very hopeful.

* * *

Fear of what was ahead faded as soon as Heather and her parents arrived at the home.

This place is beautiful, she thought, taking an introductory tour. *Nothing looks used or like a hand-me-down. They didn't spare any expense. It feels like they want me here.*

Heather had embraced the challenge of getting well and her analytical mind was processing everything around her.

We aren't allowed to talk about why we are here with other girls—interesting, Heather noted. *Most girls look completely normal. I'm curious what they're here for? But I guess it's true that no matter what got us here, we're all here for the same purpose: healing. They want good conversations and forward-looking relationships—I like that.*

Heather wasn't allowed to exercise at first, or have kitchen duty, because of her struggles with eating and exercise. At first, she was irritated by the restrictions, including the requirement to sit on the couch for an hour after meals as accountability. But she redeemed the time by writing letters to family and friends.

One day in group counseling, the girls were instructed to draw trees with roots and fruit. The fruit represented negative behaviors in their lives. Heather labeled her fruit, "Eating disorder. Restricting food. Unhealthy relationships. Need for approval." The roots of the tree represented what had grown as a *result* of the things she had experienced in her life. Heather labeled those experiences, "Made fun of in middle school. Dad's cancer scare. Date with Ryan," and a few other things. Heather's core issues—things like shame, rejection and fear— were the roots that had grown out of those experiences.

The counselor told them, "If you want apples, but you're getting lemons, the only solution is to deal with the unhealthy roots that have formed deep within as a result of your painful circumstances."

Boy, that's true, Heather thought. *I've been getting lemons for years!*

In a private session, Heather's counselor folded her tree drawing in half so she could see only the roots at the bottom of the page.

"These are why you're here," the counselor said. "We're going to talk about them."

"I thought this is why I'm here," Heather said, pointing to the fruit at the top of the page.

The counselor shook her head.

"Actually, these are why you're here, and we're only going to focus on these," she said, pointing again to the roots.

"What about my eating disorder?" Heather asked. She wanted to run directly at the problem.

"We'll get to that," the counselor said. "But first, let's talk about a negative experience that resulted in some of the damaged roots in your life."

Which one? Heather pondered. *I'll start with something less serious.*

"Date with Ryan," Heather said.

"Good. Tell me about it," her counselor said.

"It was summer," Heather began. "I was home from college. My brother's Christian friend asked me out on a date."

"What did you think about that?" the counselor asked.

"I thought, 'This is my chance to go on a date with a really good, Christian guy,'" Heather replied. "I got dressed up really nice, wore makeup, went to dinner. While we were eating, he noticed I had on my purity ring. I was wearing it for myself, to recommit to living a life of sexual purity. In the middle of our conversation, he said, 'I'm so glad you're wearing that. Girls these days don't save themselves for marriage. I'm saving myself. I deserve a virgin.'"

The counselor asked, "How did you feel?"

"Disgusted. Devalued," Heather said. "Like, 'Who are you to say that? You deserve a virgin? Like I'm some item you can inspect for defects?'"

"Let's pray through that," the counselor said. "Tell God how you felt, where you thought He was and how He saw you in that moment."

Heather closed her eyes.

"God," she began, "I feel like You were watching that situation unfold, and as soon as Ryan said that, I went from wearing a white dress to wearing a potato sack—all scratchy and ugly. I didn't think I deserved to wear a white dress. I felt unworthy. That's how I think You saw me."

Heather realized that a root of unworthiness had developed

in her life because of this interaction with Ryan—and she hadn't even known it.

"Now ask Him how He really saw you," the counselor said.

"God, how did You see me in that moment?" Heather prayed. After a moment she said, "I see me trying to take off the white dress and put on the potato sack, and I see God trying to keep that white dress on me and saying, 'You're worth this.'"

Heather began weeping. She realized that a root of unworthiness had developed in her life because of this interaction. The pain of the situation came out like a poison she had been holding inside. When she looked up after a while, the counselor was handing her a Kleenex.

"That felt good, but it was also really deep!" Heather said. "I thought I picked a safe one."

They laughed, and the session continued. The process of cutting off unhealthy roots continued week after week as Heather prayed through each hurtful life experience. One by one, she was getting perspective on those situations that had fed harmful behaviors.

I thought I was just here for an eating disorder! she thought. *It's like when you take one necklace off your jewelry stand, and it gets tangled with the others. I've been treating the eating disorder like my one necklace, but there are other necklaces intertwined that have to be untangled as well.*

Like all residents at Mercy Multiplied, Heather had to write out lies she believed about herself. She wrote, among other things:

> "I have no value anymore."
> "I am not worthy of marrying a Christian guy."
> "Food is only a reward for exercise."

"I can't trust people."
"I don't deserve good things."

Then she wrote truths to counteract each lie.

"I have great value to God, and nobody can change that."
"I am worthy of marrying a Christian guy."
"Food is made for my good. The Lord provides good and healthy things for me to enjoy."
"I can trust people."
"I deserve good things God gives."

She and the other residents independently researched the Bible to find two verses to support each truth. Then they threw away the lies and kept the cards with truth statements and Bible verses.

Heather went from barely being able to get the truthful words out of her mouth, to speaking so forcefully that she found herself actually believing what she was saying. Multiple times a day, she read those truth statements aloud, wielding them like powerful weapons to re-gain control of her thoughts.

"God highly values me!"
"I am spotless and pure before Him!"
"The Lord provides good and healthy things for me to enjoy!"
"I deserve good things God gives!"

With every statement, lies retreated from her mind and lost their power. She had never seen herself as more beautiful than through the eyes of Christ. Heather was no longer concerned with the reflection in the mirror, but with the reflection of Christ inside her. She kept the cards in her purse or back pocket and pulled them out whenever she needed them.

Mercy counselors eased her back into eating, and Heather actually became excited about returning to her optimum weight. With time, she even joined the kitchen team and became the team leader.

I was in a prison of an eating disorder, she thought, *and now I'm grocery shopping and in charge of all the recipes and planning. How amazing is that!*

One key Bible verse defined Heather's time at Mercy: Ephesians 2:10, which reads, "For we are God's masterpiece. He has created us anew in Christ Jesus, so we can do the good things he planned for us long ago." (New Living Translation)

No longer did Heather feel like an imitation work of art, continually being marked down. She knew, *I am God's masterpiece!*

Heather's parents, meanwhile, had become beloved to other girls in the house, sending letters and gift packages along with notes saying, "Tell so-and-so I've been praying for her." They also maintained a Facebook page, so family and friends could pray for Heather based on her prayer requests and updates. When Heather graduated, just before Christmas, her parents enjoyed a sweet reunion with the many girls they had supported with encouragement.

They could tell their own daughter was different, especially when she jumped at the chance to go to In-N-Out Burger before heading back to Nashville.

God has given us our daughter back, her father thought. *This is a miracle.*

Back home, Heather felt like a new person. Exercise, was restored to her—slowly.

"You need to heal your relationship with exercise," her health and wellness coach had said.

First, she was allowed to walk on a treadmill. Though it was at a snail's pace, it felt great. With goals and boundaries she progressed until she was jogging around the track in the back yard and feeling the exhilaration of running again.

To maintain her freedom, she partnered with her parents and a friend of the family for accountability and support. She was only allowed to work out with her parents at the YMCA in the morning, and met with her accountability partner every Wednesday for conversation over a delicious breakfast spread.

Within one week of being home, Heather was confronted with a major test. While seeing a movie with her family—a longstanding Christmas tradition—they emerged from the theater and ran into a group of people they knew. Among them was the guy who had raped Heather. When he saw her, he quickly looked at the floor. Heather's blood ran cold and her heart pounded.

I know this is what Mercy prepared me for—but I had no idea it would be this extreme! she thought, her breath coming in short bursts. *God, You could've waited a few more months!*

Stepping away, she walked outside and paced the sidewalk next to their car until the others joined her.

"Everything okay?" her brother asked when they arrived.

"It's alright," Heather said, but rode in silence. At home, she bolted upstairs to her room. Her mother followed a few minutes later. Heather didn't answer the knock, so her mom walked in.

"What was that about?" her mom asked pointedly.

Heather paused a moment.

"He was in that group," she said, and didn't have to explain.

Her mother sat on the bed with her.

"Okay, what do we need to do? Where are your truth cards? Get 'em out. Read them to me."

Shaking, Heather pulled the cards out of her purse and read them aloud.

> "I have great value to God, and nobody can change that."
>
> "I deserve good things God gives."
>
> "I am God's masterpiece!"

Her mother nodded, and Heather read them louder, and louder. The sound of freedom filled her bedroom, banishing the isolation and self-punishment that had bound her before. The next morning, they went to the gym, and had breakfast together as was their custom now. Life kept going, and with accountability and support, so did Heather.

This stuff works outside the home, she thought. *In the past, I would have shut myself away or numbed the pain. But I have strength to fight now.*

Soon, an email arrived advertising the local Father's Day 5K, which Heather and her dad had run in the past. She walked into her dad's office.

"The 5K is coming up in June," she said.

"I saw that," he said.

"We should do it," Heather said.

"I would love that," he replied.

Heather had begun running again and rediscovered the joy and balance of healthy exercise. Her father only ran to be with Heather, and she loved him for it. After some months, the day arrived. Early in the morning, they headed to a beautiful plantation north of town where, unlike in previous years, the course ran through the woods.

"We really should have carb-loaded at Olive Garden last night," her dad said, jumping awkwardly as he mimicked Heather's calf warm-ups.

Heather laughed. "Dad, you don't carb-load for a 5K," she said. He grinned.

"Listen," he continued as they stretched against a fence, "I know you want to stay with your old man, but I really want you to go out there and try your best. Don't wait on me. For you, a 5K is a warm-up. My goal is just to finish."

"Okay," she agreed, but wondered, *Can I do this in a healthy way? I can be pretty competitive. What if I try and don't win? Will I be hard on myself?*

The runners assembled at the starting line, and in the cool air, the gun went off. Heather leapt off the line and into a strong pace. It had rained the night before, turning the forested trail into a bit of a swamp in spots.

This is harder than I expected, Heather thought, jumping over rocks and roots, finding good footing in the soft earth. *I don't think this is what I expected when I signed up— and I don't think dad did either. I wonder if either one of us will finish?*

She saw a female runner ahead of her and set her sights on passing her. Bit by bit, she caught up with her, emerging from the woods onto the final stretch in an open field. She passed her within sight of the tape.

"Congratulations! You are the first woman to cross the line. You won!" a judge said.

No way! Heather thought. *I was just trying to beat the girl in front of me.*

Too excited to stop—and in need of a cool-down—she jogged back to where the trail came out of the woods. When her dad appeared, huffing and puffing, she ran alongside him.

"Wow, I didn't know if I would finish," he said between breaths and within sight of the finish line.

"Me, either!" Heather exclaimed. "Guess what? I won!"

"You did?" he exhaled.

"Yeah!"

"I knew I should have stayed up with you," he said.

For a prize, they gave her a gift basket with handmade pasta, sauce and a gift card to an Italian restaurant. Heather laughed.

"How ironic!" she told her family at the local pancake house where they gathered to celebrate the day. "Things I would have tossed a year ago—now I actually want them!"

But the real prize is knowing who I am in Christ, and that He has given me strength to live again, she thought, savoring the internal reward.

Victory had never tasted so sweet.

* * *

While working the early morning shift at the YMCA, Heather often greeted a guy named Daniel who came to work out. After a while, he asked her on a date. She learned he had been raised in church, had two brothers and wonderful parents.

I absolutely like this guy, Heather thought as one date led to two, and then more. *At what point do I tell him about my past, and how much do I share? I don't want to scare anybody off, and I don't want to tell someone who won't value it. Lord, if I'm to tell my story to Daniel, make it super-obvious.*

The next day, they were having sodas when Daniel said, "I've got a question. What were you doing in California?"

That's exactly the kind of opening I prayed for! Heather thought, then shared about her journey before and after Mercy Multiplied, but kept the story broad and basic. Daniel seemed understanding and unfazed.

"That must have been really hard," he said.

But as they grew closer, Heather's fear of rejection came to the surface. Sometimes she shared ugly details about her former lifestyle to see if she could hurt him, to see if he cared—and to see if he would stick around.

Why are you hurting him like that? the Holy Spirit convicted her one day.

Because I'm not used to being this close with someone, came her honest response. *I've never invested in someone like this. I want him to know me in a deep way, and I'm afraid of how he will respond.*

The next time they were together, Heather apologized for speaking out of fear, then set boundaries on sharing things with a wrong motivation. When they did talk about her past, Daniel unfailingly began with empathy and ended with grace. They were married one year after they met.

Heather had always known of Dave Ramsey from growing up in Nashville, and every Mercy resident goes through his Financial Peace University program as part of their life-skills training. Heather grew to admire his work, and the night Heather became debt-free was the very night of Mercy Multiplied's 30th Anniversary event in 2013. Coincidentally,

Dave Ramsey was the Master of Ceremonies that evening, and Heather was thrilled to have the chance to meet him and tell him, "I'm debt free!"

Little did Heather know that she would one day work for Dave Ramsey's organization, Ramsey Solutions. In 2014, Heather was hired in an entry-level sales position. She was soon promoted to the associate director of the sales support team, and as of August 2018, she is serving as an assistant to the senior director of sales.

At Ramsey Solutions, Heather has enjoyed opportunities to use her love for running and fitness in healthy ways. She served on planning committees for Ramsey Solutions' team at the Rock n Roll Country Music Marathon—driving participation and team support, and coordinating day-of cheer sites and runner initiatives. Dave Ramsey also gives financially to runners to donate to a charity of their choice. Every year that Heather has completed the marathon, she has donated money to Mercy. Dave's foundation also sponsors 5K races around Nashville, and Heather not only runs in those races, but also encourages participation from others in her company. Heather has even been approached by her co-workers for running and fitness plans and health tips.

Heather's dad wrote a poignant Father's Day letter to her, which we posted on our Mercy Multiplied website in June of 2017:

"God led you to Mercy Multiplied, and there He saved your life!" he wrote. "I remember how proud your mom and I were of you because of your diligence in following the application steps, the phone interviews, and then waiting for your acceptance into the California residence. You had to want it bad. And you did. And God led you through this process.

"Now, you're married to a great guy whom we all love. You have a wonderful job. You've kept the faith! The tears are flowing as I write this. They are not tears of sadness, but tears of joy. We are so proud of you and how far you've come. And on this Father's Day, I wanted to write you a letter to tell you that!"

That's the kind of story God is telling through Mercy Multiplied and in these young women's lives. They are indeed His masterpieces!

Heather's story reminds me that no matter how wonderful our parents and our home life may have been as children, no matter how supported and loved we may have been, no one is exempt from difficulty and pain. I have seen many examples of young women who have come into our program at Mercy, yet very few people in their world even knew they were struggling. From the outside looking in, they may have seemed to have the "perfect life", but internally, there was a battle raging.

As the old saying goes, "You can't judge a book by its cover." Most people take this saying to mean that you can't assume negative qualities about someone just based on what you see. But I believe the opposite is true as well: you can't assume that someone is healthy mentally, emotionally and spiritually just by what they portray on the outside.

Heather shares that during her time at Mercy, she began to really focus on the "inner-Heather" instead of the "outer-Heather" that was solely focused on performance and perfection. She learned about the analogy we often share of the roots and the fruit. When we have external issues we're struggling with, we often think that those issues are the problem. The truth is that those issues are simply an outward manifestation of the real, deeper problem. The unhealthy "roots" in our lives are the *source* of those behaviors that we want to see change.

Our roots draw their power from the different life circumstances that have affected us. And it's not until we expose and deal with those roots – things like rejection, fear, and shame – that we will experience true and lasting freedom.

Heather experienced the trauma and pain of being raped, and her life began spinning out of control soon after that horrible experience. Her self-image plummeted, and she saw herself as trash – "a piece of imitation artwork that was continually being marked down." The roots of her life were pain, rejection and abuse, and the fruit that grew out of those roots were alcoholism and an eating disorder.

Eating disorders are very common today, but they frequently go undetected due to their secretive nature. There are several types of eating disorders; some people struggle with one predominantly, while others bounce from one type to the next. But most eating disorders stem from deep emotional, mental, and spiritual roots, as we saw in Heather's story. Whatever the root of the eating disorder may be, the solution is far more complex than simply eating balanced meals and keeping the food down.

One of the most important keys to freedom for Heather

was renewing her mind, which is one of the main seven principles that we teach the young women in our program. You might recognize that the phrase "renewing the mind" comes straight from Romans 12:2, which tells us that we are not to be conformed to this world, but be transformed by the renewing of our minds. So the Bible tells us that when we make the choice to renew our minds, transformation happens!

Satan, our enemy, is a liar and a deceiver at his core. John 8:44 actually describes him by saying, "He was a murderer from the beginning, not holding to the truth, for there is no truth in him. When he lies, he speaks his native language, for he is a liar and the father of lies." Our enemy's native language is lying! He is incapable of telling the truth.

That's why I am so thankful that God gave us a powerful weapon to fight the lies of the enemy. John 8:32 says, "Then you will know the truth, and the truth will set you free". (Note that it doesn't just say that the truth sets us free, but the truth we *know* sets us free!) So the Word of God is the essential element of our freedom! We have to hear from God and go directly to His Word for our hearts and our minds to be renewed to the truth of who He is and who we are.

The young women at Mercy renew their minds by first identifying the lies that they have believed and then going to the Word to find truth that combats those lies. They then write out those scriptures and "truth statements" on note cards and read them out loud over themselves on a regular basis.

We can't be content to simply think these truths in our heads. It's important for our ears to hear what our mouths are saying out loud, because God's Word says in Romans 10:17 that faith comes by hearing the Word over and over again. So as we speak out loud and actually hear what we are saying about ourself, faith rises up in our heart to be able to believe the truth over the lies.

The power of renewing the mind is always a major catalyst for transformation in the lives of each young woman we work with. I can also personally testify to the power of this principle in my own life, and in the lives of innumerable others. We discuss this key to freedom in our Freedom Series resources, and we walk people through practical exercises for implementing this principle in their own lives.

One part of Heather's story that is so powerful to me is how her parents trusted God with their daughter. They did all that they knew to encourage her and love her, but they also learned that the most powerful thing they could do for their daughter was to pray for her and surrender her to God. One of the hardest things we ever have to do in our lives is surrender the people that we love the most and hold the closest. But you cannot force or coerce another person to change.

It may break your heart to see someone you love struggling and hurting, but one of the hardest lessons I have had to learn as the leader of Mercy is that if I want healing and freedom for another person more than they want it for themselves, I will not be able to help them. I can love them and encourage them. I can pray for them. But I cannot help them until they choose to seek help. They must desire change, and they must be willing to put in the hard work.

So I encourage you, if there is someone in your life who is hurting and struggling, to ask God for guidance on whether or not you need to talk to them. If so, speak the truth to them in love, and then be willing to surrender them to Him in prayer. Trust Him with them. He loves them and desires their freedom more than you could ever imagine. And my prayer for you is that you would see Jesus do a powerful work in their lives, just as Heather's parents saw Him do in hers—a story of transformation that could never be denied!

reason
THREE

Breanne

Breanne grew up in a Christian household with great parents and three younger brothers. However, when she was 12 years old, Breanne's parents moved them to a new community for her dad's new job, and Breanne was hit hard with depression and anxiety. She so feared attending public school that her parents decided that she would receive her schooling from home. With both parents working, and her brothers attending a public school, Breanne was suddenly isolated and alone. A virtual stranger in their little town that had only one stoplight, she was without friends or her former church youth group, which had been the center of her life.

With no one home to hold her accountable to doing her schoolwork, Breanne spent much of her day in bed, comforted herself with food, and watched television instead of doing schoolwork. Weight gain led to plummeting self-confidence and skyrocketing anxiety. At 12 years old, she could barely leave her parents' side in public, even at church.

Breanne also began having intense urges to keep everything perfectly clean. She began washing her hands obsessively, twice or three times in a row, using very hot water, working her nails and nail beds and finishing up with hand sanitizer. Her hands began to bleed and break open with dryness.

She feared getting her own germs on anyone or anything else. For a while, she only sat down after putting a towel down first. Using public bathrooms was completely out of the question, and when she was home, a major fear was that her laundry hamper would touch something—anything—and "contaminate" it.

Depression set in and dark suggestions came to mind: *I am untouchable and unlovable. Would it even matter if I wasn't around? Would anyone notice if I were gone?*

The thoughts escalated to, *You need to be punished for the way you are. You're a horrible kid. You have a good family, you know God, and everything has been provided for you, so why are you struggling like this?*

Breanne concluded that she was, to use the words that always ran through her mind, "worthless" and "garbage." Physically unhealthy, friendless and falling hopelessly behind in schoolwork, she decided she needed to be punished, and since nobody else would do it for her, she did it herself. She began cutting her arms. To cover the marks, she wore a black sweatshirt, even in 90-degree weather. Bitterness took deep root as she blamed her parents for moving their family.

Concerned about her lack of sociability, her parents signed her up for a homeschool volleyball league at their church. But Breanne was so overcome with anxiety that she had a panic attack in the parking lot of the church and refused to get out of the car for practice.

The only satisfaction Breanne found was in doing chores and making dinner to earn her family's love and approval—and somehow prove her value to herself.

New youth pastors at their church marked a fresh beginning when Breanne was 15. Though she had become the girl hiding in the back row—awkward, overweight, and anxious—they reached out to her and drew her into the youth group. Church came to life again. She began arriving five minutes early, then fifteen minutes, then an hour—anything to spend time in an accepting environment again.

Still, every thought seemed to accuse her: *Why didn't you sing or raise your hands in worship tonight?* an inner voice would say, and Breanne would find herself lost in guilt, even apologizing to the youth pastor's wife by text. Even worse, as the darkness and loneliness at home increased, she began considering suicide more seriously and created an anonymous email account so she could ask the youth pastor's wife for advice. The only thing holding her back was a fear of going to hell.

When the youth pastor's wife figured out Breanne was behind the emails, Breanne's parents took her to a doctor, who put her on medication and simply hoped for the best. Meanwhile, the youth pastor's wife encouraged her to pass her GED, attend a community college for a summer and enroll in a Bible college.

If I just leave this town, maybe I can leave these issues behind, Breanne thought, seizing a vision for her future. *I can move forward and everything will be fine.*

For a while, it worked. In her freshman year at Bible college, she gained confidence and made enduring friendships. She felt the Lord tell her that her career and ministry would involve relationships, but she also felt like a fraud at Bible college and didn't feel she had a personal relationship with the Lord.

A strong sense of isolation returned her sophomore year. Listening to depressing songs with negative lyrics reinforced a sense of being an outcast—and became a self-fulfilling prophecy.

Nothing's different, she decided as darkness consumed her again. *I still feel left out, hopeless. I brought all my problems here with me.*

The worse she felt, the more she refused to go out with friends. She started self-harming again, this time not as self-punishment, but as a way of trying to overcome numbness and to validate her feelings. The blood and wounds somehow made her depression seem real.

Breanne had been seeing a counselor, but when she shared about a traumatic experience from her childhood, the counselor essentially shrugged her shoulders.

That felt completely invalidating, Breanne thought.

See? said the accusing voice in her head. *You shouldn't share that with anyone. It wasn't that big of a deal. Keep your dirty laundry to yourself.*

Nothing got better. Self-harm led to hospitalization twice during the fall semester of her junior year, and Breanne almost couldn't bear the thought of her peers at school finding out.

You're at a Bible college! she told herself. *You're a Christian. You're not supposed to struggle with suicide. What do you have to be depressed about?*

She had heard of Mercy Multiplied, and the idea of applying occurred to her, but she talked herself out of it every time.

I'm not bad enough, she thought. *I don't want to take up a spot that somebody else with worse problems could use.*

All the while, she was cutting up her arms and plotting ways to end her life. Deep down was another thought: *I don't deserve help.*

When she guardedly mentioned Mercy to her friends and the former youth pastor's wife, they offered the same response: "That's a great idea!"

Breanne was shocked. *Why do people think I should do this? Maybe I'm doing worse than I thought. Maybe they're right. I know this: nothing else is working.*

Though anxious about missing a semester of school and not graduating with her class, she applied and was accepted into the St. Louis Mercy home that winter. Outwardly, Breanne was the model resident—compliant, following all rules, and quiet, perhaps to a fault. At her 60-day evaluation she expected to hear nothing but praise. Instead, her counselor's words jolted her:

"We don't know if you really want to be here."

"What?" Breanne replied, heart sinking. "I feel like I'm doing everything. I'm reading the books, doing the assignments."

"But you're not really opening up," the counselor said.

Because whenever I have opened up in the past, I've gotten invalidated, came Breanne's silent reply.

The words sunk deep into her heart. She realized she was inwardly resistant, even rebellious. God had rejected her, she believed, and Breanne was hurt and angry with Him. Not only that, she still refused to be touched or hugged—or known. Disconnection had become her default position. And when other girls spoke of finding their freedom, Breanne felt frustration bordering on rage.

How do you know when you have freedom? she wondered. *I've never felt anything like that. I don't believe it's real. I think they're making it up.*

One day a woman came to minister to the girls in a group setting and speak into each of their lives.

How can she minister to me? She doesn't even know me, thought Breanne, who prided herself on a healthy level of skepticism.

The minister stood before her praying and said, "God wants you to feel like the whole room is hugging you right now."

You've got to be kidding me, was Breanne's first reaction.

"You have felt love-starved," the minister continued, "but

you are loveable. And God is giving you eyes to see the good ending in things. You are a bondage-breaker to help others break free."

Breanne's heart was pounding now. Skepticism had given way to vulnerability in about two seconds.

Oh, my gosh, she thought as the woman continued to speak. *Is this really happening? I can feel this is true, and she's speaking directly to my soul and my future. Is this what freedom feels like?*

Pictures of her future came to mind, of Breanne counseling and helping others, similar to what God had showed her in her freshman year. Somehow, she also felt known and validated by God, no longer guilty for experiencing such deep depression and anxiety. The ministry time was recorded, and Breanne listened to it over and over.

As she did, and as daily Bible study and counseling continued, lies were exposed and replaced with truth. She was able to replace the lies that she was worthless, untouchable and unlovable with the truths that she was worth more than she could imagine, made to have close relationships and built to receive and share God's love. With a new passion, she pursued a relationship with God and forgave herself for the lies she had believed and the choices that she had made. God showed her that her relationship with Him was not based on what she did, but on what He had already done for her.

On top of that, Breanne was overweight when she entered Mercy and lost sixty pounds while in the program. Healthy eating, exercise, and good lifestyle habits made a huge difference and brought major self-confidence.

"You're there," a staff member told her. "You've made so many incredible changes."

"You just told me a couple months ago that I wasn't there!" Breanne replied, amazed again at how others saw her so differently than she saw herself.

The staff member smiled.

"You're full of hope and fully empowered to walk this out," the staff member said. "You have everything you need."

Without missing a beat, Breanne graduated from Mercy Multiplied, then returned to Bible college, took summer classes, and was able to graduate with her class. A mentor encouraged her to attend graduate school, and in an accelerated program, Breanne earned her master's degree in clinical mental health counseling. The girl who once had no hope and wanted to take her own life finished the master's program in 18 months and was named the most outstanding student in her program—a total life change.

Breanne also traveled to Africa twice to offer counseling care. There, God stretched her and pushed her beyond what she thought was possible. She realized how much she could do with God leading the way and giving her open doors and strength to do His work.

Today, Breanne works for a child and adolescent psychiatric residential treatment facility in Indiana. Children ages 6 to 18 spend several months to a year on the locked and secure campus, each struggling with some kind of disruptive or life-controlling behavior. Breanne conducts individual, group, and family therapy sessions and gets to live life six days a week with the residents. The problems they bring—suicidal thoughts, self-harm, aggressive behavior—are not for the faint of heart, she says, but Mercy so impacted her with its example of effective residential care that Breanne wants to multiply the result from her own life into the lives of many others.

After Mercy, she continued walking out her freedom and lost more weight until she was a healthy size again. She also serves as a youth leader at her childhood church, pouring into kids' lives and sharing her story when appropriate opportunities arise.

"I was the shy kid who sat in the back of the room and dressed in black, and had a lot of bad stuff going on that nobody knew about," she told them recently. "These problems happen in your church because they happened to me."

Then she told them how she found freedom through Christ at Mercy Multiplied.

"I want to impact and change people's personal worlds," Breanne says. "Mercy Multiplied and many others impacted my world. I want to do the same."

————

Breanne walked through the doors of Mercy with her head bowed low, covered in shame. She felt hopeless and alone. She believed the lies that she was unlovable and untouchable.

Because Breanne thought she was "garbage," she had been harming herself physically. Many people think that self-harm comes from someone's desire to take their own life. And while suicidal thoughts may accompany self-harming behaviors, they are often very different. Self-harm is ultimately an outward expression of pain and hurt deep within.

It's so important to remember that the roots of our self-destructive behaviors must be dealt with and removed in order to experience true and lasting freedom. When Breanne was younger, self-harm was a form of punishment for being "worthless." Breanne struggled with deep shame over who she was and over her struggles, and her shame made her feel that she deserved punishment. Shame is relentless, often grabbing you and holding on for dear life.

As Breanne grew older, self-harm shifted from being a form of punishment to being a means of overcoming the numbness that she felt emotionally. Desperate to feel something, anything, the pain of each cut became a reminder that she was, at least, alive.

When Breanne came to Mercy, God started bringing light to the darkness and showing her the lies that she was believing. He started replacing those lies with the truth that she was worthy of love, that her life was worth living. She was able to work through the pain of her past and allow God to bring a deep level of healing into her life. As she allowed herself to actually feel pain, the door opened for her to start feeling *all* emotions again – including joy and peace. As Breanne was able to truly feel again and no longer believed that she was "garbage" and needed to be punished, she wasn't compelled to self-harm anymore. When her roots were exposed and uprooted, the life-controlling behavior no longer had a place to grow.

Another important part of Breanne's journey was in learning how to forgive herself for her past choices. The enemy, who is also known as the *accuser*, had heaped so much shame and condemnation on her. As a child, she had believed that she was a "horrible kid," and as she grew older she thought that she shouldn't be struggling since she was a Christian.

But when she came to Mercy, Breanne learned that the Word of God said He keeps no record of her wrongs. She learned that, according to Psalm 103:12, "As far as the east is from the west, so far has He removed our transgressions from us." Breanne learned that all God asked of her was that she recognize her sin, confess to Him, and commit to turn from that sin.

Some of us may be able to accept and believe the fact that God has forgiven us, but like Breanne, we have a hard time forgiving *ourselves*. We may feel as if we are more in control and even experience a sense of safety by remaining angry with ourselves, but that control is deceptive. We must learn to fully receive God's grace but also to extend that grace to ourselves.

The most amazing thing happened the day Jesus died on the cross: God's judgment toward all of the sins we have ever committed and all of the sins we will ever commit were placed on Jesus. When we give our lives to Him, we have to start believing we are who God says we are. He tells us that in Christ, we are forgiven, free, and pure, and the enemy cannot make unclean what God has made clean! Forgiving yourself is no easy task, but the freedom that follows is incredible.

We also see in Breanne's story that she struggled with anger at God when she came to Mercy. She felt hurt and rejected by Him. She had experienced a great deal of pain in her life—some due to life circumstances and some due to her own choices. But Satan had convinced her that God was the source of her pain. The enemy told Breanne that God had rejected her and abandoned her.

One of Satan's greatest tactics is to deceive us into thinking God is the author of evil things that happen. It is one of the enemy's deadliest tools because if we think God caused our pain, we will never trust Him to be the Healer of our pain.

When people who have been hurt hear that God has a plan for their lives, they often say, "If God's plan looks like what I've experienced, I don't want anything to do with Him." I want to be clear with you, though: There are two plans for your life. God has a plan for you, and the enemy has a plan for you. And they couldn't be more opposed to one another.

I call John 10:10 a "dividing Scripture", because it clearly states that it is the thief (the devil) who comes to kill, steal, and destroy, but that it is *Jesus* who stated that He came to give us abundant life. So what that means is that anything on the side of "kill, steal, and destroy" is not from God. It clearly states in Psalm 119:68 that God is good, and that He does good. It also states in James 1:17 that every good and perfect gift comes from God.

When Breanne started to understand the truth of God's good heart towards her and His good plans for her life, she was able to trust Him again. She learned that God is perfect in love and had only done good to her. It was never His desire for her to be hurt and rejected.

Still, it is easy for people to get caught up in the why: "Why did this happen to me? Why did God allow it?" The answer is simple: Someone did evil to you, you chose evil for yourself, or evil simply happened because we live in a fallen world. The good news is that God did not abandon us to this evil, but rather He came to redeem us from it.

God's love for you is so great that He sent Jesus to pay the penalty for your sins. His heart was broken, so yours could be healed. Now He wants to give back to you everything the enemy has stolen. Once again, God is not the Author of your pain; He is the Author of your deliverance and freedom.

It is amazing to see how God delivered Breanne from the

lies and depression that had defined her life prior to Mercy. He restored her trust in Him. He restored her joy and her life. No one can argue that Breanne's life has been radically transformed by the power of Christ!

reason

FOUR

Kittie

Kittie was born on the Fourth of July, so everyone down at the bar her father frequented called her "Firecracker"—an appropriate nickname for a fiery, petite young girl growing up in Nashville. As a toddler, Kittie spent evenings playing among the barstools, enjoying the social energy of the adults and listening to the up-and-coming country bands that played there. When it got late, she curled up in her dad's office and fell asleep.

Back home, things were less harmonious. At a young age, Kittie sensed her mother's instability, and when her parents divorced, when she was three years old, she was happy to learn she would live with her father. For a while, things were good. He made homemade food and embraced his role as a single parent. At the bar, he was popular and funny, and had more friends than Kittie could count.

Things got rocky when he started bringing girlfriends home. When one serious relationship broke up, he slid into depression and reached for the bottle. A shadow fell across Kittie's childhood. Time at the bar was spent entertaining herself with her dog, Belle, and creating a garden out front. Her dad's good humor always disappeared by the time they got home. Sometimes she heard him sneak out after she was in bed to go drinking again.

Kittie had dreamed of being a motivational speaker, but now her personality turned inward. She made bad friends and was kicked out of school in seventh grade. To get a fresh start, her father moved them to Memphis, but his depression and drinking came with them. Kittie avoided the house.

A group of older friends became her sanctuary, especially a boy named Brian. His family was welcoming and stable, and his parents let Kittie stay at their house to escape her home environment. Their consistency was a saving grace, and Brian's loyal friendship a strength, especially after she was kicked out of the private school her uncle had paid for her to attend.

Following in her parents' footsteps, Kittie began smoking marijuana at the age of 13. At sixteen, she became pregnant by a boy at school who had just received a full scholarship to a major university.

I can't tell anyone, she thought. *This will destroy his life. He has a future—I don't. I'm always in trouble and going down the wrong path. Plus, I'm just sixteen. I can't afford a child.*

Choosing abortion laid waste to Kittie's soul, and emotional pain drove her to harder drugs. Her friend, Brian, began using heavily because of Kittie's influence, and his bright future started slipping away, too.

Two years later, at the age of 18, fully entrenched in a shared addiction, Kittie became pregnant again.

I can't have another abortion, she thought through the haze of dependency. *There's no way I can justify it this time. It's too much guilt to go through again. But neither I nor Brian are stable enough to take care of a child. And the drugs—what will they do to the baby?*

Numb and focused on staying high, she chose to have a second abortion. The trauma threw her into a full-blown heroin and methamphetamine addiction. For four years she hung around the worst people in town, committed crimes to feed her habit, and was barely surviving.

Kittie was arrested and charged with her first felony (forgery of a check from her sister) and was sent to jail at age 23. Her pod was 13 rowdy girls sharing metal bunk beds in a room entirely made of concrete. Kittie received a top bunk because she was young and small. Bottom bunks were for the older ladies. Their mattresses were tiny. Lights were left on all night, forcing them to craft eye masks from ripped sheets. 23 hours a day they spent in the pod, one hour in the yard.

Kittie received a Bible on her first day there, and with little else to do, began reading the gospels. The Bible hadn't interested her in the past, but now it came alive. She was captivated by Jesus and the idea that He came to save people like her.

That is so profound, the possibility that Jesus could do something with my life, she thought, staring at her prison cell ceiling. *I wonder if it's really true? Could He help someone like me?*

A voice inside seemed to respond, *There's a plan and purpose for your life, and it's so much better than what you've been doing. If you turn it over to Me, I can do what I desire, but you have to let it all go.*

She pondered what the voice said, then rolled back over and continued reading. The Bible brought peace to her in the middle of all the fights and disunity in the prison. At times, just opening it seemed to calm down the entire pod.

Kittie collected sticky notes, scraps of paper and yellow pads of paper from the commissary for journaling and letter-writing. She often wrote to her dad, who did not visit as much as she wished. She wrote to her cousin, who had been bugging her to apply to a place called Mercy Multiplied for several years, and whom Kittie had always ignored and avoided in her addiction. And she wrote to Brian, who was there every visitation day, loyal even while his addiction gutted his once-promising life.

But most of her writing was about God.

God is real, she journaled. *He is here with me, and somehow He is going to use all of this for good in my life.*

I feel God's presence wherever I go. I have peace I can't

explain because my outside circumstances are not peaceful at all. Wherever I go, He is paving the way.

He set me apart. There is something greater beyond these walls. I feel free for the first time. Despite being in physical chains and captivity, I am starting to get a taste of true freedom on the inside.

I once was lost and now am found, was blind and now I see. The veil has been removed. I know the truth.

Kittie was so excited to find out that there was a Bible study being held inside the prison walls and a church service that she could attend on Sunday mornings. She even recruited other women to go with her.

But back in her bunk, dark thoughts about Brian often clouded her hope. When they had first met, he was almost entirely clean, enjoying a good home and a healthy family. Now he couldn't hold a job or go to college because of the drugs Kittie had introduced him to. He even wrecked his car while driving high.

Who do you think you are, turning your back on your lifestyle when you helped destroy his life? an accusing voice asked. *You have to be loyal to him and the others. You got him into this—you see it all the way through.*

Tormented by guilt, she fell into restless sleep.

The violence and monotony of jail life was broken by the occasional ray of sunlight, sometimes in the form of one of the guards. One female guard seemed of a different spirit than all the rest—kind, even smiling, and offering bits of advice and encouragement that stuck with Kittie.

"If you don't have something encouraging or uplifting to say about another person, then don't say anything at all," the guard said one day, and though it was in passing and could have been easily forgotten, Kittie wrote it down in her journal.

How does this woman have such joy in here? she wondered. *She carries herself differently than anyone else.*

Some rays of sunshine were literal as Kittie earned a coveted job cleaning the bleachers and dugouts at a local baseball park. The job didn't pay, of course, but it took her and several other women outside of the prison walls for a while. While Kittie swept up trash, she prayed, "God, please help me when I get out of here. I'm going to need a lot of things—a car, a place to go, some new friends. I can't do it on my own."

The two-hour round trip to the park in the prison van gave her the luxury of silence. She would lean her head on the window, take in the beauty of the passing scenery and picture her future.

Seven months after entering the prison, Kittie was released. But freedom from the prison bars became a hell like no other.

Unable to stay away from using, and haunted by what she had done to Brian's life, Kittie started working for escort services to pay for her habit, as she had done before going to jail. Now, the crushing emotional pain from escorting drove her to live with a prominent drug dealer just to supply her habit and get her off the streets. She was surrounded by crime, large-scale theft and abusive behavior.

This guy is certifiably crazy, she often thought of her dealer. *But what else can I do? I don't want to be sober, and I have nowhere else to go to stay off the streets.*

The peace she had found in prison was gone, and nothing in her present lifestyle was bringing it back.

One day the drug dealer she lived with dropped Kittie off at a friend's house, then ran a stop sign and was followed home by police who found his house full of stolen goods. He was sentenced to seven years in a federal prison. Kittie knew it was more than coincidence that she wasn't with him at the time of his arrest.

Waking up one morning in a dirty house after a long drug binge, she knew she was done. She grabbed her phone and called her cousin.

"I'm ready," Kittie said. "I'm ready to apply to that place."

* * *

Almost 3,000 thousand miles away in Manhattan, Dave, the son of a New York City fireman, had bottomed out. Justifying every step along the way, he had abandoned a successful athletics career in high school to move from one drug to another: marijuana, acid, pills, mushrooms, and cocaine. Using led to selling, and selling to arrest. He was a convicted felon before turning 20.

While serving time on probation, and working as a plumber, he began abusing painkillers and, finally, heroin.

I'm a full-blown junkie, he thought while driving in his car one night. *When I was doing marijuana, I promised myself I'd never do pills, then crack, and now heroin. I've blown through every one of those promises. All I do is bow down and submit to this syringe.*

In a moment of transparency, he asked his family for help and found himself at Long Island Teen Challenge, a faith-based program for drug addicts. During his first night there, Dave prayed, "God, if You are who my mother says You are, and You can help me get rid of this addiction, I'm all in."

Teen Challenge utterly transformed Dave's view of Christianity—and Christian men. Some of the men at his childhood church had struck him as soft and feminine. Through the example of his mentor and other guys around him, he realized he could play sports, lift weights, laugh and joke around, and love Jesus with all his heart. God built a new foundation for Dave based on new, healthy relationships. He graduated from Teen Challenge in October of 2010.

Out in California at the Mercy Multiplied home, Kittie was receiving deep inner healing for a decade of painful behavior. But at first, she found it extremely difficult to speak to her counselor. Her drug use had brought anxiety and fear of speaking in front of anyone, even one-on-one. During counseling sessions she remained silent and let her mind go so that she did not feel present in the moment.

Patience yielded results as counselors slowly walked her through the healing process and spoke truth to replace lies. Kittie's choice to make a *total* commitment to Christ washed away the guilt of her past. Soon, Kittie was getting up early each morning, before anyone else, to sit in a chair in the library, read the Bible and spend time alone with God.

Seek first the kingdom of God—I live by that verse, she wrote in her journal. *In seeking Him, He will resolve all the things I am worried about: the healing and restoration in my own heart and in my family, and where I am to go after graduating from Mercy.*

Any time God spoke to her in a clear way, she wrote it down and labeled it "A letter from God." It usually was about who she was in His eyes. Before long she had filled several journals with biblical and personal promises, and daily reflections and prayers. Truth statements, replacing lies with truth, became her arsenal against fiery darts of accusation. She often walked around the basketball court in the back yard speaking the Scriptures out loud.

"This is truth. I am a child of God. No weapon formed against me shall prosper. Lord, give me faith that no matter where You send me, whatever You have me do, without even thinking about it, I will go. You are in control."

Toward the end of her ten months there, a strange thing happened during worship time. An old patriotic tune kept coming to her mind: *From California to the New York island* ... At first she was annoyed by the interruption.

Why is that song in my mind? she wondered. *I haven't heard it since preschool.*

Worship continued. But the little line from "This Land is Your Land" kept coming back to mind.

From California to the New York island ... From California to the New York island ...

After a while, Kittie caught on.

This isn't just random, she realized. *I've never been to New York, and this is not something I would normally start singing in my head. God, is that from You?*

A sense of peace was the only response. Tentatively, she told some girls in the program, and when their faces lit up, it provided another confirmation. One of them said, "My dad's a pastor. I'll ask him if he knows anyone in New York."

Within weeks, Kittie was invited to attend Long Island Teen Challenge and then serve as an intern there after her time at Mercy. Just as the song said, she flew from California to New York the day after graduating.

It seemed that God was determined to provide more training in public speaking as Kittie was called on to share her testimony often at the house and at local churches. The first time she was so scared that she stood for two full minutes without saying a word.

I can do all things through Christ who strengthens me, she told herself, repeating the truth statements she had memorized. Then, with a deep breath, she began.

"My name is Kittie. I'm from Tennessee, and I love Jesus . . ."

Soon, she was invited to help pioneer a women's Teen Challenge home in Albany, New York.

I feel like this is my calling, she wrote, *to be with the women at that home, ministering and teaching them. Thank you, Lord!*

In Albany, she met Dave who was now the program manager at the men's home and was helping to renovate the facility. He spent days ripping up sub-floors, laying carpets, painting rooms and updating the plumbing for the entire house.

She's the sweetest thing in the world, Dave thought during one of Teen Challenge's services. *The way she worships the Lord is so genuine and heartfelt. That's the type of woman I would want, if I ever got back into dating.*

Without being too obvious about it, Dave found reasons to come to the women's home to do maintenance, and offered to grocery shop for them as well. One day a friend in the program called him.

"Yo, normally I don't do this stuff, but the rumors are that Kittie likes you," the friend said.

Dave's heart skipped ahead a few beats.

"That's cool," he replied calmly, "but I'm not dating anyone right now."

Why am I being so stubborn about this? he asked himself.

A week-long trip to a leadership conference in Virginia Beach solidified his feelings as he was given a chance to get to know her more.

Afterward, he thought, *It's only been two days and I miss her. That's a telltale sign. I must have genuine feelings for this girl.*

He asked for a meeting with his executive director, who welcomed him in with a grin. He seemed to know what was coming.

"Well, Dave," he asked, "Any girls you're interested in?"

Dave stuttered and replied, "I've taken a notice of Kittie. I'd like to get to know her a little."

In Teen Challenge, staff members needed permission to date. The director smiled bigger and said, "You have our approval."

With their courtship officially beginning, Dave discovered they had very different approaches to getting to know each other. Kittie was reserved, cautious, building trust over time. Dave was much more open to talking about anything and everything.

He was also deeply angered by what people had done to Kittie in the past.

God, I'm not sure I can forgive these people for their actions, he prayed, seeking guidance.

She has, the Lord reminded him.

That simple realization made the difference. Kittie's own freedom became Dave's freedom as her mercy softened his heart. *How could I hold onto anger and bitterness towards these people if she has released them?* he asked himself time and again.

Getting to know Dave, Kittie saw that his sense of humor, his character, and his love for God and for the guys in the program was deep and real. And his love for her was growing.

Dave planned a special proposal, under the Christmas tree in Rockefeller Center in Manhattan. For some reason, he had envisioned the moment being more private, but instead, every visitor in the northern hemisphere seemed to be in New York that night. Nerve-racked, he handed his phone to a random couple to take their picture, then to Kittie's surprise, he got on one knee by the ice-skating rink.

"Kittie, I love you, and I want to spend the rest of my life with you," he said above the noise and bustle. "Will you marry me?"

Kittie beamed. "Yes!" she answered as they hugged.

Just a couple of months after the proposal, Dave was sent to Buffalo, New York, to serve as the program director at the men's Teen Challenge center there. Kittie stayed in Albany and continued to work at the women's home while planning their wedding.

Kittie and Dave were married in late June of 2017. The women in the Teen Challenge program helped Kittie set up and decorate for the wedding and the rehearsal dinner. A few of the girls in the program were even able to attend the wedding, which was very special for Kittie. Her parents and other family members attended as well.

Standing next to Kittie that day as her matron of honor was the cousin who had told her about Mercy, and her maid of honor was a close friend who had been in the Mercy program with Kittie. The two had stayed in touch since their graduation from the program, and were just one of many examples of lifelong friendships that have been built between Mercy residents. Kittie and Dave were in awe of how God honored their marriage through the many blessings of that day.

One year later, Dave now directs the men's Teen Challenge center in Buffalo, New York, and Kittie fulfills the administrative roles. They have built it from 5 students to 26, raising local support for the house and teaching men to pursue Jesus and his call on their lives.

"I use the tools I learned at Mercy throughout our program every day and have yet to come across a more organized, well-run, and fruitful ministry as Mercy," Kittie told us. "I strive every day to bring that same level of excellence to the ministry my husband and I now have the privilege of running."

Kittie now speaks with great confidence in any setting, and is enrolled at a Christian college to earn her bachelor's degree in psychology. With further training and biblical foundations, she wants to spend her life helping women get free from their pasts and embrace all God has for them, just as she learned to do at Mercy.

———————

Kittie's story reminds me of how someone can know about God and know His Word, but still walk in bondage. When Kittie was in prison, she studied the Bible, attended Bible studies, and even journaled about God and sensed His nearness. However, when she was released from prison, she found herself back in a dark pit from which she couldn't seem to escape.

It's heartbreaking to think about how many people know God, even people who have committed their lives to Him, yet still live their lives in chains. In our study, *Keys to Freedom*, we use the analogy of a kettle that is plugged into the power source, but the power is turned off. It looks like a kettle and has the potential to boil like a kettle, but until it is switched on, it is powerless. We can look like Christians by going to church and Bible studies, but if our lives are disconnected from the power source, Jesus Christ, we will miss the truth, power, and freedom that He died for us to have.

Kittie's story teaches us that a *total* commitment to Christ is required. When Kittie made the choice to go "all in" in her relationship with Jesus, things in her life started to powerfully shift. If God reveals to you that something is getting in the way of your total commitment to Him, it's time to let it go. Not some of it—all of it.

God has given you a choice between life and death, captivity and freedom. If you want to be free—really free—you need to come to a place of complete surrender and commitment to Christ. You need to connect, perhaps for the first time, to the power source for living life in freedom and wholeness. If you have never done so, I encourage you to make a total commitment to the only One who can truly set you free: Jesus. (There is a Prayer of Salvation included in the back of this book if you'd like to make that commitment right now.)

Kittie shared that her choice to make a *total* commitment to Christ is what washed away the guilt of her past. One of the enemy's greatest weapons is shame and condemnation. He tries to convince us that we didn't just make a mistake; we *are* a mistake. The shame of the abortions, the condemnation of her bad choices, the guilt of how she believed she affected her friend, Brian's life. It was all weighing heavily on Kittie's heart when she entered the Mercy home.

But when Kittie made the choice to fully commit her life to Christ, she was able to receive *all* that He did for her, which included the washing away of her sins. She walked with confidence that she was truly *in* Christ, and she learned about how Romans 8 says that there is "no condemnation for those who are in Christ Jesus." The enemy wanted to keep Kittie stuck in the shame of her past, but when she learned the truth about those who are in Christ, she was able to lay her past at Jesus' feet and walk away pure and spotless. As 1 John 1:7 says, "the blood of Jesus his Son cleanses us from all sin."

I love in Kittie's story how God spoke so intimately and personally to her. She began sensing His voice while she was in prison, and when she came to Mercy, He spoke to her heart in powerful ways through the Holy Spirit. I wholeheartedly believe that God's primary means of communicating with us is through his Word, the Bible. Hebrews 4:12 tells us that the Word is living and active. It has the ability to change our hearts, and it always has something to say about our lives. The Word is our ultimate standard of truth, but it is not the *only* way that God speaks to us. One of the most awesome gifts that we are given as His children is the ability to have two-way communication with the Father through the Holy Spirit. True healing and freedom is not possible outside of the presence and truth that God communicates with us through His Word and through the Holy Spirit.

Outside of Scripture itself, God may communicate to you in many different ways. It might come as a thought, a memory, a picture, or a verse from the Bible that comes to mind. It doesn't necessarily mean that you hear an audible voice from heaven; it just means that the Lord shows you something, and you receive what He is communicating to you. Jeremiah

33:3 says that we can call out to God and He will show us things that we do not know. Throughout Scripture, the Lord promises to speak to us and reveal Himself to us, but the Word also serves as the standard of truth and a compass for anything that we believe we receive from Him in prayer. (If the concept of hearing God's voice is new to you, I encourage you to check out our Freedom Tool on the Mercy website entitled "Hearing the Voice of God," which can be found at MercyMultiplied.com/Freedom-Tools.)

One of my favorite things about Kittie's story, along with countless testimonies of other Mercy graduates, is how she began a generation of blessing through the power of her choices. The truth is that we are all predisposed to becoming what has been modeled to us, and Kittie had started to fall in line with many similar lifestyle choices that her parents had modeled to her. We often adopt our parents' and grandparents' approach to life—both the positive and negative things—sometimes without even realizing it.

But there is good news! Through Jesus' blood, a new bloodline was created that we enter when we choose to accept His salvation. When you are in Christ, the power to change is in your spiritual bloodline! In John 3:5-6, Jesus tells a man named Nicodemus, "No one can enter the kingdom of God unless they are born of water and the Spirit. Flesh gives birth to flesh, but the Spirit gives birth to spirit." When we come to Christ, we are born again by the Spirit. We enter into the family of God through the bloodline of Jesus Christ, and His blood is stronger than the blood of our earthly families. The blood of Christ has the power to break every negative pattern that comes down to us by genetics or habit.

Kittie's story reminds us that in Christ, the power of generational patterns is broken! God has given us the power to identify and reject patterns in our family's history and establish new patterns that bring blessing to our future and to the futures of those we influence. When we identify a negative pattern that has been handed down to us, we must first surrender that pattern to God and then exercise the authority and power of choice that flows from our spiritual bloodlines as sons or daughters of God. We can then ask Him to replace that negative pattern with a generational blessing!

What you plan and purpose in your heart today will affect the generations that follow you. As we share in *Keys to Freedom*, "It's not all about here and now; it's also about then and them, those who are in your future." Kittie's life was powerfully transformed by the love and power of Christ, and there is no telling how many lives will be affected by her choice to pursue freedom. Just like Kittie, your choice to pursue freedom today will affect other people's tomorrows! I like to put it this way: "Who is on the other side of your obedience?"

reason
FIVE

Monica

Monica's parents met in South Korea, where her mother had been trafficked and sold into a brothel as a teenager. Her father, serving in the Air Force, was struggling with drug and alcohol addiction when he met the 17-year-old girl, fell in love, bought her freedom and brought her back to the United States. They married—he was 19—and had two daughters, Monica and Jessica, within two years. Their mother could barely speak English.

As the girls grew up, their mother showed every sign of severe PTSD, and their father was rarely present. When he was, he was high or drunk, though not violently so. Any semblance of parenting or nurturing was absent. Monica wore a house key around her neck from the age of seven and cared for herself and Jessica while their parents worked. Paychecks went to drugs. The family bounced from one apartment to another, and the girls were regularly forced to change schools. By adolescence, Monica didn't feel loved, known, or capable of attaching to people in a healthy way. She smoked her first cigarette at age 12 and started experimenting with drugs at 13. Jessica began drinking at the same time.

Their mother had found God through the knock of a stranger at the door of their apartment in Seattle. It came after a prayer: "God, if You're out there, help me," and His response seemed to be a woman who showed up randomly to invite them to a local church. Without thinking it through, their mother asked her to come in and promptly broke down crying.

"May I pray with you?" the woman asked, and their mother agreed. Holding hands and listening to the petitions, she felt hope for the first time in her life. From that day forward, she dragged the family to church on Sundays. Though the girls gritted their teeth and rolled their eyes, it was deeply impressed on them that there was a personal God Who cared for them. Their father, meanwhile, excused himself halfway through every service and waited for them in the car.

One day when Monica was 17, her father summoned her to the garage.

"I need your help," he said. "I'm afraid your mom's going to leave me."

"Why?" Monica asked.

"She says I need to go to treatment," he said.

"What kind of treatment?" Monica said.

He walked over to the car and pulled out a duffel bag. Opening it before her, he revealed masses of syringes and needles stuck together by a sticky, revolting substance. Monica had never seen that kind of drug paraphernalia. Her jaw dropped as she stared at the ugly sight.

"Heroin," he said. "Black tar heroin."

"Whoa," was all Monica could reply, and her heart felt squeezed with anguish. Her father had hidden it so well. He went to work every day, came home at night, and showed few outward signs of addiction, aside from constant financial debt and lack of emotional connection. Monica soon learned that her sister had once caught him shooting up.

His time at treatment didn't last long, and their mother, unable to cope with his addiction, left anyway. He began using openly in front of his daughters in the house, drinking alcohol with them and giving Monica drugs, including cocaine.

A month after their mother left, Monica came home to see him passed out on the couch and her sister screaming.

"He's having seizures!" she said. Next to him on the floor was a bottle labeled "Valium."

ER doctors rescued him from his suicide attempt. Back home, Monica pleaded, "Dad, we need you. Mom's gone. You've got to stick around."

A week later he didn't come home from work. At eight o'clock the hospital called. Someone had found him in an alley, facedown, beat up and not breathing. Paramedics started his heart with a defibrillator. Fresh needle marks dotted his arm. All brain activity was absent.

While driving home alone from the hospital, 16-year-old Jessica cried hysterically and called out to God.

"Look, God, I need You to wake him up," she said. "Wake him up!"

Out of nowhere, she heard a crystal-clear voice inside say, *I will be with him whether he decides to stay or go, but I will be with you always and I will take care of you.*

Their father died three days later.

Now completely on their own—their mother had fled the entire situation—Monica and Jessica bounced around, living with family and friends. For Monica, college acceptance offered a new start, but things quickly deteriorated. She sought out the most broken kids and joined them using heavier drugs. Though highly intelligent, she failed her classes, moved back to Seattle and for five years lived as her father had: working during the day and using drugs at all other times. By now, she and Jessica had drifted into separate worlds.

At times, Monica called Jessica for help, like on Christmas day at 5 a.m.

"I don't know where I am!" she said, voice trembling. "I'm scared. Come get me!"

Jessica and a couple of friends got into the car, drove an hour to Seattle, managed to find Monica and brought her to their apartment. When she had rested up, Monica left again. That was their relationship for years.

Finally losing her job and apartment due to addiction, Monica overdosed a couple of times, then went on a five-day binge with no sleep.

If something doesn't change, I will die, she concluded.

For the first time, she fell on her face and cried out to God.

"If You're real and You want me to live, You have to do something, because I can't," she said. "I can't do this anymore, but I don't know how to stop."

A family friend had mentioned Mercy Multiplied, and though cocaine still ruled her, Monica filled out and sent in the application. Medical tests showed that she was pregnant. Having suffered two abortions already, Monica strengthened her resolve.

"I am having this baby," she promised herself.

Instantly, she stopped desiring drugs. The need to use lifted. There were no more crazy urges, no detox symptoms, no wildly swinging emotions, no cravings.

I finally have something to live for, she thought, feeling a measure of peace. *That in itself is a miracle.*

Two days after discovering she was pregnant, Monica was approached by a woman she knew from a local church.

"We heard you were pregnant, and though we don't know the sex of your baby, we bought you something anyway," she said. "Do you have any inkling what you're having?"

Before thinking it through, Monica blurted out, "It's a boy and his name is Samuel." She opened the gift box: inside was a blue piggy bank, perfect for a boy.

I think God is rescuing me through this pregnancy, she thought. *I wouldn't have quit using for anything else.*

79

Monica arrived at the Nashville Mercy home angry and walled-off to relationships. At age 24, she had been fending for herself for 17 years, and any rules felt restrictive.

Seriously? I have to stand in line for my pre-natal vitamins? she fumed. *I have to check out a razor and return it because some girls choose to cut themselves? The staff tells me when to go to bed, when to wake up, when to eat, what to eat. I'm not sure I can handle this for long.*

Outwardly she supported the process and even took on a big sister role with other girls, but soon the process of uncovering repressed emotions, and the hard realization of what had become of her life, pushed her to desperation. Worse, a pinched nerve in her back was causing great physical pain.

Okay, God, I'm here, she said as she entered class that morning. *I don't feel like being here, but here I am.*

As worship began, she bowed her head and prayed deeply.

God, Your Word shows what real life and real freedom look like. I want them, but I feel so far from them. All I can see is what I messed up. I'm hurting in all sorts of ways and I'm frustrated that I can't change anything—not even this stupid pain in my back!

Suddenly, an intense aroma of lilacs filled her nose.

Whoa! Where is that coming from? she wondered. *Someone's perfume? Or an oil? What's going on?*

The fragrance began to move from her nose down into her body, and when it reached her back pain, her back became very warm. The pain disappeared.

Oh, my gosh, she thought. *This is amazing. I'm being healed!*

The intense warmth, the smell of lilacs, and the feeling of complete acceptance, peace, joy and physical wholeness lasted for minutes. Monica cried with gratitude, and during the sharing time that followed, she testified to what had happened. Everyone applauded as Monica cried for joy.

The healing and emotional changes accelerated. Monica now felt grateful that, for the first time in her life, she had been given life-giving boundaries and limits. They brought safety and were an expression of love. Counseling, too, became a place of greater healing, and she appreciated God's gentleness with her through the process. Bit by bit she learned how to build healthy relationships with God and others.

One day, out of curiosity, she looked up the meaning of "Samuel," the name she had chosen for her unborn baby. One meaning, she learned, was "Because I asked You for him." Chills ran down her body.

That's me, she realized. *I got what I asked for—a reason to live and to beat my addiction—and I named him before I knew what it meant or if he was a boy. God really does love me and want the best for me.*

Samuel was born on September 27, 2005, and Monica's mother, with whom she had begun to reconcile, flew in for the delivery. Monica graduated from Mercy Multiplied two days later and moved in with her mother and her mother's new husband in Chicago.

Job opportunities brought Monica back to Nashville when Samuel was two years old. Monica went to school and focused on building a solid career. She worked her way to the top of every high-profile sales training organization in the city. She eventually found herself in upper level management, making enough money to send Samuel to a great private school.

From the start, Samuel's life seemed especially blessed.

Monica watched as God lined up the right people and opportunities for him year after year. She was amazed at how the Lord took care of them and was sure that He was blessing her for choosing life.

Monica was intentional about staying in community with godly people. She believed strongly in the law of sowing and reaping, and she tithed diligently. Year after year, she experienced exponential increases in life.

In 2015, Monica was reconnected with a man she had dated five years prior, a record executive who was managing a large country music act. Within one month, they were engaged and six months later were married. He adopted Samuel.

Meanwhile, in Washington state, her sister, Jessica, was soaring professionally and floundering personally as she worked for an aerospace company. Counseling hadn't helped sort out her past, and neither did the constant flow of alcohol and prescription drugs.

Her nightly routine was set in stone: Get home, change straight into pajamas, sit in front of the computer and idly surf, pour herself one drink after another, mix in prescription pain relief and muscle relaxant pills, drink to the point of vomiting, come back out to the computer and start drinking again.

One afternoon, as Jessica was very drunk before the sun had gone down, she did something rare and dialed Monica's number. The two had been estranged for years.

"Hello?" Monica answered. Jessica came to tears almost immediately.

"I can't keep living like this," she said. "But I don't think there's anything I can do to get out of it."

Jessica had observed from a distance how her sister's life

was stable now. She even seemed to be flourishing. Monica listened for a while, then offered a final suggestion.

"Let's pray now," she said.

That's weird—we've never prayed together before, Jessica thought, *but then again, everything is weird right now. I'll just go with it.*

"Okay," she replied, and Monica prayed a simple prayer that God would intervene in her sister's life.

The next night, Jessica sat down at the computer, poured herself a tall glass of wine and took a drink.

Huh, she thought. *Not that good.*

She took another drink. *Maybe I just don't want wine tonight,* she thought and dumped it down the sink, poured a glass of Scotch and sat down again. The Scotch tasted just as bad.

I have no desire to drink anything, she realized. *Oh, my gosh, what an unfamiliar feeling!*

From that day forward, her boozing ended and she never touched pills again. But God wasn't finished. Days later, her relationship with her boyfriend fell painfully apart. While Jessica sobbed, a small, familiar internal voice said rather calmly, *This is exactly what you asked for. This is your opportunity.* She stopped crying immediately and said aloud, "I've got to go." The next day she gave her notice of resignation at work, terminated her lease, donated many of her possessions to a thrift store and began the process of moving to Nashville to live with Monica.

Today, both sisters live in freedom, with families and fulfilling careers. At 36, Jessica is happily married with two small children. Jessica is now teaching philosophy at a large community college near Chicago. Her husband earned a

degree in systematic and historic theology and is now a pro-
fessor in a local university's Department of Humanities and
Theological Studies.

Monica creates pottery, and she and her husband are
remodeling the home they recently bought. Samuel continues to grow and excel in his pursuits.

Both sisters point to how God used Mercy Multiplied—
one directly, one indirectly—to rescue them from self-
destructive behaviors.

"Even in our worst moments, God's hand has been on
our lives and He won't depart from us," Jessica says. "Regard-
less of the crazy things we have been through, He's been
faithful."

I will never forget when Monica walked through the doors
of Mercy in March of 2005. As her story revealed, she had a
major drug addiction and cried out to God for help. That is
when she made the decision, at the urging of a family friend,
to apply to our Mercy Multiplied program and get the help
she so desperately needed.

Part of the process of filling out the Mercy application
is that medical tests are required. It was in this process that
Monica found out that she was expecting a child. Monica pre-
viously made the choice to have two abortions, but this time
she knew she wanted to make a very different choice. She
wanted to choose life, not only for her baby, but also for herself.

Many years ago, when various groups of people were

picketing at abortion clinics and blocking abortion clinic doors, I felt like God showed me that I was not to be a part of these activities, but rather use my time to provide an *answer* for these young women. God showed me that He did not want me to block abortion clinic doors and get arrested and thrown in jail, but rather open our residential facilities to actually provide a practical way for a young woman who wants to choose life to come in and be cared for during the time of her pregnancy.

In that process, our job is to care for her spirit, soul, and body, and allow her to go through Basic Decision Making classes to determine if she wants to parent or to place her child for adoption. In the event that she chooses to parent, our job is to prepare and equip her to be the best mom that she can be. Likewise, in the event that a young woman would like to place her baby for adoption, we allow her to make a complete list of what she would like in an adoptive couple, and with the help of our Director of Adoptions, she is allowed to make the final decision about who that adoptive couple should be.

I am so thankful to tell you that since we made the decision to take in and care for young women facing an unplanned pregnancy, hundreds and hundreds of women like Monica have walked through our doors. We have had the privilege of honoring the choice of each young woman, whether it be parenting or adoption. We have placed hundreds of babies in adoptive families, but like Monica, we have also prepared hundreds of others to be exceptional mothers.

Many years ago I began to seek God about showing me a counseling model that could be used in all of the Mercy homes. In that process, God dropped into my heart a counseling model containing freedom principles that we now refer to as *Choices That Bring Change.*

Monica's life is absolute proof that positive choices today will bring about positive results for tomorrow. Her biological family set her up for a generational pattern of family dysfunction, addiction, and premature death. While Monica was in the Mercy program, she committed her life to Christ, and realized that God had given her the opportunity to receive freedom from all the pain and bondage of her past.

Monica realized she could receive a new beginning in life when she heard the scripture in 2 Corinthians 5:17 that says if any person be in Christ, they are a new creation. In God's eyes, old things have passed away and all things are new.

We also shared with Monica what it says in Deuteronomy 30:19, "This day I set before you life and death, blessing and cursing. Choose life so that you and your seed may live."

Monica got a personal revelation about what this scripture actually means. She did not realize that she had a choice about what her future would look like. She had been told her whole life, "Once an addict, always an addict. Once you're this, you'll always be that." As a result of her revelation from this powerful scripture, Monica made the choice to choose life and to break the old generational patterns and start a generation of blessing.

Rather than keeping the identity of a "recovering drug addict," she boldly proclaimed her identity as a new creation in Christ. Monica made the choice to no longer identify with the past problem but rather her new identity as a child of God who has been set free.

Instead of walking in bondage, Monica became a conduit of freedom. As a result, she impacted her sister, Jessica, to the point that Jessica eventually made the same choices that Monica made and received her new life in Christ. Today, both Monica and Jessica are living and walking in freedom and enjoying beautiful relationships with their husbands and children. The old generational patterns that once existed have been broken in both of their lives, and today they are experiencing the generation of blessing as a result of the choices they made to follow Christ.

It has been one of the greatest joys of my life to watch Monica's life be transformed, not only during her stay at Mercy, but since the time she walked out of our doors with her baby boy in September of 2005. Monica's reconciliation with her mother was a beautiful thing, as the power of forgiveness flowed and their relationship was restored.

I was super excited in 2007 when I found out that Monica and Samuel were back in Nashville because I knew that meant that I would get to see them often. I love having them in the same town!

The first thing that was so fun for me to watch was the very successful business woman that Monica became. She had amazing job opportunities and went from promotion to promotion because of her gifts, talents, and abilities.

Beyond that, my favorite thing of all was seeing what an amazing mother Monica was to her son, Samuel. She was able to provide for him above and beyond as a single mom, and she patiently waited for God to bring the right man into her life. When she and her husband married in 2015, he immediately adopted Samuel. Now 13 years old and thriving, Samuel and his mom are very, very close, and he also loves his dad.

Since being back in Nashville, Monica has been very involved with Mercy Multiplied on a number of levels. She and her husband have hosted tables at fundraising events, and they have also personally given to Mercy financially.

Monica has also been an active volunteer with us in several different ways. She has shared her story at Mercy luncheons for new friends and supporters both in Chicago and Nashville. Monica has also been very generous in sharing her story in the Mercy homes to encourage residents who are where she was back in 2005. What a tremendous blessing this has been to so many young women!

Monica also volunteered to be part of recording a parenting video to encourage pregnant Mercy residents who are in their decision making process. In addition, Monica chose to record her personal testimony video for Mercy, and she was also included in one of our Mercy promotional videos.

It is so fulfilling for me and my staff to see all that God has done and continues to do in the life of Monica and her beautiful family. She represents thousands of others whose lives have been radically changed, and her life speaks so loudly that it doesn't need words.

reason
SIX

Heather

Heather was a soccer-playing, fun-loving kid who grew up in a Christian family near Washington, D.C. One day when she was 12, two boys who lived nearby and were a little older began teaming up to sexually harass her at the bus stop. She spent bus rides shoving them away, telling them "no" and looking out the window in hopes that ignoring them would stop the behavior. None of it worked. Strangely, nobody else on the bus intervened, so their daily "game" went on all year. Emotionally wounded, Heather concluded that this was the way the world worked. Anger and confusion clouded her heart, but she kept it all inside.

In eighth grade, a stranger on a social media site sent her a message introducing himself and saying he wanted to make friends on the site.

Cool, Heather thought hopefully. *I need someone to talk with, too.*

The two began messaging back and forth every day, sometimes for hours. Heather knew little about him except that he lived in her town, and that he was older than she. Sometimes the conversations were simple and light: "How was your day?" "Good. How was yours?" At other times, anonymity allowed her to pour out her heart more openly.

This guy really cares, she thought. *He's so interested in my life.*

She had a large circle of friends at school and on her travel soccer team, but the online friend seemed more mature and understanding. She could talk to him in a grown-up and logical way, and he responded sympathetically.

One day, she received a message from a girl online who knew the same guy. This girl said she really liked him, but that he was interested in someone else. Heather knew she was the "someone else," but said nothing. Soon, the guy's messages took a new turn: "I'd love to meet you one day." "It'd be fun if we ran into each other sometime." Eventually, he proposed meeting somewhere, but Heather, who was just 14, politely declined.

He went silent. Heather checked for messages after school, but there weren't any. Her heart was troubled.

He must be mad at me, she thought. *I haven't heard from him in a week. What did I do wrong?*

The local news soon revealed the answer. The man, who was actually 45 years old and had teenage daughters, was arrested by the FBI for transportation of a minor across state lines for prostitution. Officers had stepped in before any sexual acts were performed, so they could only charge him with "intent". The victim was a 16-year-old girl. The location was a hotel restaurant. FBI agents contacted Heather's father and said they had reason to believe the man was preying on Heather as well.

Oh, my gosh. I was talking to a predator this whole time, Heather realized. The news report didn't show his face—just his fake profile picture. His jail sentence was two years.

Two years! That's it? she thought. *I don't even know what this guy looks like. What if he gets out and comes looking for me?*

Terrified, she quit sleeping in her own bed or bedroom because, by her logic, *People get raped in their beds. I'll be safer if I'm not even in my room when he comes for me,* she thought. Night after night she dragged her blanket and pillow to the sofa downstairs, or to the living room floor. As she lay there in the dark, every noise sounded like a man coming to prey on her.

The guilt was crushing. *That girl who messaged me online— was she his victim?* Heather wondered. *Shouldn't I have done something? But how could I? I didn't know he was a predator. Still, he tried to victimize me, but he got her instead. I'm responsible for what she went through.*

Men, she concluded, were untrustworthy by nature. They wanted to use women in a sick, sexual manner. No one actually cared.

Heather's parents deactivated her social media accounts and forbade her from using the computer unless someone was standing directly behind her. But they didn't realize how much communication there had been, or how deep the relational roots had grown. Now Heather was consumed with fear. *Is he stalking me? Does he know who I am? Do I know his kids?* Though her family environment was healthy enough, she found it difficult to bring up painful things.

Afraid to venture into public alone, Heather colored her hair blonde and cut it short as a kind of disguise. But it didn't relieve the emotional pressure inside. One day while sitting on her bed doing math homework, her ankle kept itching no matter how much she scratched it. Finally, in frustration, she raked her pencil back and forth across the spot. Dots of blood appeared on her skin. *Oh, my gosh—I made myself bleed and I didn't feel pain,* she observed. *In fact, I feel calmer and weirdly relieved.*

The false feeling of comfort seemed to solve some of the churning confusion, so Heather began cutting herself every couple of weeks, mostly on her ankles where the wounds could be hidden with tall socks. The self-harm seemed to offer a sense of power and control over her emotional pain and her body that nobody could take away.

She extended that harmful power over other aspects of life, including eating. Anxiety had robbed her of hunger, and she began deliberately going days without food. The discomfort of fasting pulled her mind off the fear of her online predator finding her.

During her sophomore year, 11 friends and family members died in a span of eight months—both her grandfathers, parents of friends, and several classmates who committed suicide. One classmate, her best guy friend, Christian, died in a hunting accident. Heather found herself in funeral homes every month, including on her 16th birthday.

In a tailspin of grief, her self-harm escalated. Her friend Christian had loved food—burgers, fries, Slurpies at 7-11. Heather decided, *If he can't eat, then I won't either.* Withholding food was a distraction from thinking about losing him and the others. When her stomach growled and her head spun from lack of nutrients, it took her mind off never seeing them again. At one point, she consumed nothing but water and Diet Coke for eight straight days.

In the winter, layered clothes kept people from noticing her weight loss. But in the warmer months—and on the soccer field or track—it was harder to hide. Her athletic performance suffered, and soon she had to give up varsity sports to accommodate her controlling habit. She started skipping school regularly, or sleeping in class, or sitting on the locker room floor for long hours to avoid the classroom. She was failing her honors classes.

Binging and purging up to nine times a day, then fasting long stretches and cutting her body, drove her to a mental breakdown. Heather experienced her first anxiety attack at school, blacking out, waking up and not knowing where she was. When she figured it out, it happened again—black out, wake up, wonder where she was. Soon she was shaking, crying, sweating, hyperventilating and blacking out repeatedly.

After a trip to the emergency room, her parents entered her into a treatment program. She had harmed herself to the point of needing stitches, and had carved the word "hate" into her ankle twice, along with her online predator's initials into her arm.

I do hate myself, she thought. *I'm the reason this is all happening. My life's getting worse and worse. I know I'm destroying myself from the inside-out by not eating, and from the outside-in by cutting. But I don't care.*

The treatment program closely monitored the girls' eating, checking their napkins for hidden food and always accompanying them to the bathroom. But it didn't seem to help. At the end of eight weeks, Heather experienced a day-long anxiety attack, believing that her online predator was after her again. She ended up strapped to a stretcher in a white hospital room with padded walls.

"You're getting worse," the hospital personnel told her. "You have to go somewhere else."

Heather went home with her parents on the condition that she apply to a long-term facility. Their pastor recommended Mercy Multiplied, but Heather left the application in her room and tried to solve the issues on her own. The result was more visits to psychiatric in-patient facilities, one of which kicked her out for being "a bad influence" on the other patients.

After achieving a small measure of fragile stability, Heather tried to re-start her life by attending a university two hours away. There, life bottomed out. Relieved to be away from her hometown and her online predator, she instead found endless freedom to cut, binge and purge all day. Insomnia from anxiety drove her to an impossible cycle of 52 hours awake and 4 hours asleep. Then, multiple anxiety attacks, which came with little warning, forced her to medically withdraw from university.

"You need electro-convulsive shock therapy," her next therapist recommended.

That's crazy, Heather thought. "What if I lose my memory?" she asked.

"Would it be that bad if you forgot the things you are unable to heal from?" the therapist asked.

Heather considered it. *I think my options have narrowed down to being dead, or being alive with no memory,* she concluded. At age 19, she began a regimen of electro-convulsive shock therapy three times a week. Probes on her brain induced seizures. The idea was to rewire her neurotransmitters, like restarting a computer. After ten rounds, she lost a year of memory and a noticeable amount of her daily vocabulary.

Aside from the memory loss, there was some improvement in her stability, and for a few weeks back home, her family felt that the old Heather had returned. Then she received news that a girl she had met at a treatment center was murdered for drug money while in Florida. While they weren't good friends, Heather had no coping skills left and her eating disorder and self-harm returned with a vengeance. She found herself in the ER again for self-inflicted wounds, malnourishment and dehydration. Her parents, who had already put locks on the refrigerator and pantry doors to prevent binging, and locked the bathroom doors to prevent purging, didn't know what else to do.

At that moment, Heather was given a clear view of her life.

I'm a story of defeat, she reflected. *I let these events break me down and tear me apart. I don't even feel like a human being anymore. I'm on 12 psychiatric medications. I have no personality, no life. I can't even do daily things. I need something else or I won't survive.*

At Heather's request, the family's pastor met with them, and he spared no words: "The only way you will change is by coming to Jesus," he said. "It's a relationship, not a religion. Then you need to get help from people who put Jesus first—and you can beat this. Let me ask you, Heather: If God could use your situation and what you have gone through to stop a girl from going through what you went through, would it be worth it?"

Heather burst into tears unexpectedly. "Yes, of course. Even one person would be worth it a hundred times over," she said.

"Then you have to be the one to take steps to change that," the pastor said. "Your dad gave you that application to Mercy some time ago but you never sent it in."

"I filled it out!" Heather countered.

"But you didn't send it in," he said, firmly yet gently. "Secular treatment misses the main focus: Jesus. He is the One who will change your life."

That day, Heather mailed in the application. She was accepted and her parents drove her 12 hours to the Mercy home in Nashville. Her first impression was that there were no rooms with padded walls or beds with straps on them. *That's a good sign,* she thought. Indeed, the place seemed beautiful and peaceful, with pleasing furniture and colors and gardens.

"You're here on an unusual day," said the woman who greeted them in the lobby. "We're going into a graduation ceremony in about an hour. We don't usually do intakes on graduation days."

Heather and her parents gathered with others in a packed room to celebrate the residents graduating the program. They looked beautiful, all dressed up and with their hair done. Then they began sharing their testimonies—and their words hit Heather's heart like a hammer.

If these girls hadn't told us what they had been through, I never would have known it just from looking at them, she thought. *It's amazing to see them standing there sharing these crazy stories, yet looking so normal and healthy.*

Whatever hesitation remained melted away in that God-appointed moment.

But Heather's first three months at Mercy were rough. Initially, she hid food in her napkin or cut it into tiny pieces and threw it under the table. She was surprised that staff didn't stand over her while she ate or accompany her to the bathroom. She realized that getting better was going to be her responsibility.

Nobody's breathing down my neck here, she thought. *If this is going to work, I have to want it. How badly do I want to be free?*

After a while, she stopped hiding food, and she never purged at the home.

But she still refused to sleep in a bed. She was only able to sleep if she was on the floor, or leaning against the dresser watching the door. Anxiety drove her to always be facing the easiest way out of the room. Even then, she could only function by taking three sleep-inducing medications.

For a while, Heather didn't advance much in counseling. One day her counselor excused Heather from the group with the suggestion that she go to her room and pray about what was holding her up. The counselor said, "You have to move on and know you're not an evil person. Ask God why you can't forgive yourself."

Heather went to her room and got facedown on her floor.

"Why can't I forgive myself?" she asked aloud.

God's response seemed clear in her heart: "Why do you feel like you need to? Did you do anything wrong?"

Heather thought about it. "No," she said. "Actually, I don't really know."

"Take a step back and consider the logical approach," God seemed to continue. "You didn't go to jail. You didn't stalk anyone. You didn't harass anyone on the bus. You don't need to be forgiven in this situation because you didn't do anything wrong."

Strong feelings of false responsibility welled up in Heather's heart to counter His words.

But I'm a bad person, a troubled child, the black sheep, she thought. *I'm dirty, disgusting, undeserving. That's why men target me. I'm the common denominator in these situations. I draw terrible people to myself. And what about the girl who met up with the online predator? That was my fault, right? She took my place in the victim line.*

"No," she sensed God respond. "You are none of those things, and none of those situations were your fault."

"None of it?" Heather asked.

"None."

An oppressive weight seemed to lift off her soul, and for the first time in many years she glimpsed freedom.

"Okay," she prayed. "You're God, and you know. If you say I didn't do anything wrong, then I didn't."

She stood up feeling like a different person than the one who had come into the room. In a few moments with her Heavenly Father, everything had changed.

Personal counseling uncovered other lies. Heather had always believed that she was not angry about what had happened to her. In fact, she realized, she was very angry.

That is so bizarre, she thought. *I didn't think I was angry because I don't scream or stomp my feet. But I've lived in anger for nine years, and it turned into self-hatred inside of me.*

Counseling also taught her a proper grieving process, the value of sharing how she was suffering with those around her, and asking for help. More than anything, she began to really believe who God is, and how big of a sacrifice He made for her. During teaching sessions, Heather embraced discussions and dove deep into journaling her thoughts about the Bible.

God, I see what You're saying here, she would write, *but this other thing is what I have believed my whole life. How can I take this biblical truth and apply it well so I can move toward freedom?*

It took time for the lies to be exposed and broken down, but when the anxiety attacks stopped, she knew she was getting free.

She also got closer to sleeping like a "normal" person. With the permission of Mercy's Director of Medical Services, Heather dropped her sleep medications one at a time. At night, she sat up in bed reading until she got tired, then moved to the floor. Each night she tried to stay in bed a little longer. One night she was listening to music and reading and fell asleep sitting up in bed. The next day she burst into her counselor's office, beaming.

"I didn't do it on purpose, but I slept in my bed," she announced. "I did it! I actually slept in my bed."

Her counselor celebrated the huge victory.

Heather actually rediscovered what falling asleep naturally feels like. At first she didn't know what was happening because she hadn't done it in so many years. Now she laid her head down on the pillow, let her mind wander, and dozed off until she was fast asleep. She couldn't remember the last time she had experienced that wonderful, God-given process.

Praise and worship times were some of Heather's favorites, including spontaneous moments when they were sitting around and someone brought out a guitar to play. *This is the coolest thing,* she thought. *Can I bring you all home with me?*

One evening, another major bridge was crossed. It was bedtime, and the whole building was quiet when Heather marched into a counselor's office.

"I think I want a family," she stated.

"Okay. That's cool," the counselor replied.

"You don't get it," Heather said. "I have never trusted anybody, much less a man, much less the thought of an intimate, married relationship. I have been okay picturing myself as an ER nurse, working midnight shifts and serving other people. But until today I never thought I would have a family or trust a man enough to have a family with him. Now I know: I want a family."

"That is amazing!" her counselor said, and gave her a high-five.

Still, it came as a surprise when, a few weeks later, Heather's counselor gave her a graduation date.

"Excuse me, I'm still struggling with some things here," came Heather's response. "I won't make it in the real world. We haven't even started to talk about a lot of what I've been through. Every other counselor and therapist wanted to resolve all those feelings and situations."

"Everybody's healing is different," her counselor said. "Maybe that's not your way of healing. It's not always about unpacking every detail about the events themselves, but addressing the emotions and the lies that you believe as a result of the events. And anyway, you still have time to put in work."

Heather sighed. "Okay," she said. "You're crazy, but I trust you."

It turned out to be true. Breaking the lies of false responsibility had unchained her from the past. *This is amazing,* Heather thought. *I don't have to go through and pick every situation and moment apart. I just changed what I believed about the situations and myself. Now I have peace—real peace. I went through those things, but it's not who I am.*

In other programs, she had been told that she would need long-term treatment for Post-Traumatic Stress Disorder and that she'd never be able to live a normal life. Heather realized in her time at Mercy that this was not true. God healed years of hurt with the presence, power and truth found in Christ.

Heather graduated from Mercy in August of 2013. Graduation day was busy, a whirlwind of reunions and fun as she welcomed her parents and a friend to the home. Heather was a little nervous but so eager to share her story of life transformation. Three other residents graduated with her that day. When Heather's time to share came, she stood up and said, "I'm going to focus more on the change God has made in my time here and less on why I ended up here." She did just that, giving God all the glory for rescuing her from life-controlling behaviors.

In the audience, her father and mother cried, and when the microphone was passed around for friends and family to share their thoughts, her dad raised his hand. The room fell silent as he paused, and tears rolled down his face.

"Heather," he said, "the devil stole nine years of your life." The tears on his cheeks grew bigger as he struggled to continue: "I'm just so glad they've been restored."

* * *

Back home in Virginia, Heather found a job at a veterinarian clinic, cleaning kennels. The young man who trained her, David, took notice of her.

She's different, he thought. *Selfless, really caring and helpful to other people. I don't think she's ever complained, even when we have to stay late.*

They eventually began dating, but while David was falling for Heather, she was on a slower pace. For one, she was suffering physically from the damage done to her stomach during her eating disorder. Tests and doctor visits peppered her schedule, but no one could figure out her mystery diagnosis. Eating caused great pain, so her diet was mainly limited to dietary supplement drinks.

Though David brought flowers and foods she could eat, and sat on the couch to watch television with her in the evenings, Heather felt tired and weak. She often went to bed before sundown, and at one point told him she needed a break from their relationship.

"David, don't give up. You'll get there," a mutual friend at the vet clinic told him. "Keep being persistent. Walk with her through this and things'll work out."

One day, when their relationship was back on, Heather showed him a thick binder of medical papers.

"These are all the doctors I've seen in the past two years," she said. The reality of her journey hit him.

This girl is amazing, he thought. *She holds down a job, goes to doctor's appointments all the time, and deals with me, and yet she seems so peaceful. What kind of guy am I? I complain if I have a rough day.*

Heather's faith had deeply impressed him. As any good boyfriend would, he had started attending church with her, mainly to win over Heather's father and pastor. But he found himself drawn to worship and the solid Bible teaching.

Then one day the pastor pulled him aside.

"I know why you're here," he said. His tone was direct but not accusing.

"What do you mean?" David asked.

"We all see the way you look at her," the pastor said. "Heather is very special, and she has been through a lot. Be good to her."

Gulp, thought David, examining his own heart. For as long as he could remember, his creed was simple: Do good things, and good things will happen. But that seemed shallow compared to Heather's devotion to Jesus Christ. And it didn't change his often self-centered motivations. He had spent most of his life chasing pleasures and money, even if that meant burning people along the way.

Under the microscope of the pastor's scrutiny, David kept coming to church and seeking out conversations with the pastor and Heather's father. His heart began to turn away from worldly things and toward the truth he saw manifested in their way of life.

I want the kind of relationship with the Lord that Heather and her dad and the pastor have, he thought. *I've been so focused on my stuff, doing everything for me. I've been oblivious to the main reason we're here: to serve the Lord.*

One day after a significant conversation with the pastor, David decided to spend time praying in his living room. As soon as he hit his knees, he started crying. It was only the second time he remembered shedding tears.

"I'm sorry for how selfish I've been," he said aloud, "all the people I've hurt, all the stupid things I've done."

Joy washed over him in great waves, and an overwhelming peace, even as the tears flowed freely.

All my past is gone, he realized. *I don't have to be that way anymore! I feel so at one with the Lord right now. Why have I been waiting my whole life to do this?*

Later that day he told Heather, and she jumped up and down with excitement. Not only did David experience a miracle, but Heather did too. Her normal appetite returned, and a normal relationship with food had been fully restored.

The day David proposed, he took Heather to special places in their journey, then to her house where her family had decorated and lit candles for the moment. With Heather smiling and blushing, David got down on one knee and stammered, "W-w-will you marry me?"

Through tears, Heather replied, "Yes."

The bonds of friendship formed by residents at Mercy often run deep, and many of Heather's "Mercy sisters" stood as bridesmaids in her wedding in September of 2016.

Today, David regularly speaks at their church, giving mini-devotionals that he studies out from different books of the Bible. The timidity he felt about public speaking has gone away. He is bold in his faith, telling everyone he can about the Lord. Gone, too, is his former tough-guy image. Now he wears a big smile all over Loudon County where he serves as an animal control officer.

Heather rose to a leadership position at a pet hospital where she works part-time as a veterinarian assistant. She is also a full-time college student earning all A's in pursuit of her nursing degree.

The scars on Heather's arms and legs have mostly faded, and most people have no idea about her past. Sometimes she meets people who seem to be struggling with emotional problems or life-controlling issues, and she invites them to coffee, to share her story.

It's a story of the ultimate strength and hope available to any one of us in Jesus Christ.

———————

We often think about sexual predators as roaming around playgrounds or hiding behind bushes, but in today's world, predators search for victims while hiding behind a computer screen. People—especially children and teens—who are willing to communicate with strangers online are easy prey for predators.

The Internet offers something that predators didn't have in the past: anonymity. Ernie Allen, former President and CEO of the National Center for Missing and Exploited Children said, "Predators are hiding behind the anonymity of the Internet to target kids, to entice kids online—to try to persuade them to meet them in the physical world."

This is exactly what happened to Heather. She unsuspectingly started an online conversation with a seemingly innocent man. The anonymity allowed her to pour out her heart openly, though, and their relationship grew closer and deeper. She had no idea that she was being pursued by an online predator.

I am so thankful that God protected Heather. Had she chosen to go and meet this man, her story would have been much different. Unfortunately, we hear of people drawn into these types of situations every day, and sometimes they even lose their life. It's heart wrenching, and we're on a mission to help people understand how dangerous it is.

It's heartbreaking to imagine that in the midst of all her pain and fear, Heather lost so many friends and family members over the course of her sophomore year of high school. The grief was more than Heather could bear. When tragedy struck in her life, the enemy seized that opportunity to bring her into even deeper bondage.

Grief is a huge problem that many people are facing today, but it's important to know that there is a difference between a normal grieving process and a spirit of grief that attaches itself to someone who is hurting. The normal grieving process includes denial, anger, bargaining, depression and acceptance. People who are grieving don't always go through each of these stages in the same order or even experience all five of the stages, but this is a very normal process that someone walks through when they experience a loss. During her time at Mercy, Heather actually had to learn what a proper grieving process looked like.

Certainly any one of us would rather avoid the valley of pain, but to short-circuit this process would be to rob ourselves of experiencing God's healing power. When people don't walk through the grieving process after loss, a door can be opened for a *spirit of grief* to take hold in their lives. For example, my family experienced a horrific tragedy when I was a young child, but we never dealt with the loss; we simply bottled up the pain. Because no one helped us walk through the grieving process, there was an overwhelming, and almost unbearable sadness that gripped our hearts for years. We stuffed the grief as we all went into our individual coping mechanisms to deal with the pain. This allowed a spirit of grief to take hold deep within us.

We know from Psalm 147:2 what the heart of God is towards people who are hurting: "He heals the broken in heart and binds up their wounds." In my case, it required a professional Christian counselor as an adult to get through this process. You may want to consider Christian counseling or pastoral help to navigate this process well.

In Heather's story, we read that she was on 12 different psychiatric medications at one point and that one therapist suggested she needed electro-convulsive shock therapy (ECT). ECT is a procedure in which small electric currents are passed through the brain, intentionally triggering a brief seizure. The procedure is used to cause changes in brain chemistry to attempt to reverse symptoms of certain mental illnesses. However, after ten rounds of the treatment, Heather lost a year of memory and even part of her daily vocabulary, and it only took one piece of bad news for her to spiral out of control again.

It's fascinating to me that one of the answers that the world gave to Heather was a process that could literally cause her to lose some of her memory. While the world might suggest that we *lose* our minds, God's Word tells us that He wants to *renew* our minds. When a young woman enters the doors of one of our Mercy homes, our desire would never be for her to lose part of her memory. Instead, we encourage her to allow God to bring His perspective and His healing to the painful memories of her past. We encourage her to partner with God in renewing her mind to the truth of who she is and who He is. It's through the healing and renewing process, not the *removal* process, that true freedom is found!

It breaks my heart when I read about how much self-hatred Heather had toward herself because of the things that had happened to her. She was filled with so much shame and condemnation, and the enemy had actually convinced her that the painful circumstances she had experienced were her own fault. Many victims of abuse or trauma blame themselves for the things that others did to them. They believe that it's all because of something they did or didn't do. But I would like to set the record straight here and say that no one is ever to blame for the abuse or mistreatment upon them by other people. Ever.

Heather believed that she was "a bad person, a troubled child, the black sheep." She thought she was "dirty, disgusting and undeserving" and that this was why men targeted her. Since she was the common denominator in each of these situations, she assumed that she was to blame.

While at Mercy, though, Heather learned that she was not the cause of the things that had happened to her. When she allowed the Holy Spirit to speak to her heart and reveal the truth to her, she shared that a huge oppressive weight was immediately lifted off her soul.

If you are personally struggling with self-blame for the painful actions of other people, I encourage you to recognize false responsibility. Who owns what and where does your own personal ownership lie? You are responsible for your own thoughts, feelings and actions, *not* those of another person. Release yourself of the responsibility of others' actions, and ask God to speak to you about who you truly are as His child.

Heather had been told by many different treatment programs that she would never be able to live a normal life and that she would need long-term treatment. But I love how, in six months' time, God miraculously healed years of hurt through the power of Christ. Heather didn't leave Mercy perfect, but she did leave transformed. And the Holy Spirit is continuing to complete the awesome work that was started in Heather's life. I love how at her graduation, Heather wanted to focus more on what God had done in her life than what had happened to her in her past. She epitomized what Isaiah 43:18-19 encourages us to do: "Forget the former things; do not dwell on the past. See, I [God] am doing a new thing!" Heather is a beautiful example of a life that has been made new by the love of God and the power of Christ!

reason

SEVEN

Nicky

Nicky's early childhood near Boston was marred by sexual abuse. The abuse resulted in deep feelings of shame and anger, and the belief that her shame needed to be hidden. Nicky's parents divorced when she was eight years old, and she experienced relief but also confusion. She was hopeful that things would get better, but instead they continued to feel unstable.

Nicky started looking for ways to numb the pain from the abuse and the divorce. The emotions that she felt were too overwhelming, so she sought to find things to mentally disconnect from the experiences. She felt that she couldn't control the circumstances and her own emotional responses, and as a result, she developed an obsession with her body image at age ten, which led her to skip meals, purge and exercise excessively. At 13 she began cutting her arms, waiting until her family went to bed, then sitting in her closet with paper towels to catch the blood. As she did, she watched herself in the mirror.

I hate myself so much, she thought as the routine seemed to focus and calm her racing thoughts for a while.

Gymnastics and cheerleading were Nicky's joy. Skilled at movement, and blessed with an outstanding local team, Nicky excelled at high-level acrobatics and stunts. She stood in the back position during cheer routines and caught the "flyer"—the girl thrown high into the air—by her shoulders, back and head. Nicky's own flips, back hand springs, and front and back tucks looked as natural as walking. The intense teamwork, the rush of competing, and the precision of two-and-a-half minutes of choreographed dance and cheer routines gave Nicky a sense of community and accomplishment that nothing else in her life matched.

But when not at cheer practice, she used other things to try to numb her pain: underage drinking, pot-smoking and sexual activity beginning in middle school. Depression weighed on her like a heavy blanket, keeping her from forming real relationships.

Plummeting grades brought meetings with a guidance counselor, who noticed the scars on Nicky's arms and called her mother, Kim. Kim was floored.

I don't even know what cutting is, Kim thought. *Why is Nicky doing this?*

A psychiatrist diagnosed Nicky as bipolar and prescribed medications. Nicky promised to stop self-harming, but instead became more secretive, carrying her arms in such a way that the marks were harder to notice. By age 15 she was drinking alcohol frequently, cutting herself nightly, skipping meals, binging and purging, smoking cigarettes and marijuana, sleeping around and considering suicide. Friends became distant, alarmed by her behavior. Nicky filled journals with dark poetry chronicling her lifestyle in painful detail.

As a high school freshman, Nicky experienced the high point of her cheer career when her team won county and state competitions and advanced to the final tournament, held at Disney's Wide World of Sports arena. There, Nicky continued restricting food and purging, but found the competition exhilarating. Though it hurt to catch the flyer in her self-wounded arms, Nicky performed at her peak. At the culminating ceremony, all teams sat on the competition floor, holding hands and waiting to hear who won. Nicky's team was named the top team in the country, and received their trophies amidst a flood of tears, cheers and the strains of "We Are the Champions."

But elation only lasted so long. Back home, the emotional pain somehow seemed worse.

Why am I in such agony? Nicky asked herself guiltily. *I don't have a reason to be like this—I have a good mom and step-dad, and brothers and sisters. But I can't stop feeling this way, and that's my fault. Everybody wants me to change and I don't know how.*

Nicky's parents had divorced when she was eight years old, and her mom had remarried and had three more children with Nicky's step-dad: a four-year-old, and twins less than a year old. Family life had improved greatly, and Nicky's secretiveness, while perplexing to her mom, Kim, seemed like a mark of adolescence, or a personality difference. Kim knew her own mind was more logical and methodical, while Nicky was more creative and passionate. And as a young mother in her early thirties, Kim was doing her best to figure out parenting.

One day a male high school friend of Nicky's, who often drove her home and gave her cigarettes, followed her inside the house and raped her. After that, Nicky's eating disorder went into overdrive and she starved herself for a week—except for a single piece of candy for lunch each day—then tried to overdose on aspirin. Her cheer coach discovered the suicide attempt, and Nicky was taken to a hospital in Boston, then to a psychiatric ward for minors where Kim and her family left her overnight while awaiting more direction from the doctors. The ward was darkly lit and completely devoid of furniture or objects of any kind, except for mattresses on the floor.

I can't believe I just left my child there, Kim thought on the way out. *I don't know what's real and what's not real anymore. I feel like my life with Nicky is a lie. What I see isn't the truth with her—so what is?*

Nicky's typical life—including her cheer career—faded away as she cycled through hospital visits, residential treatment centers, psychiatric units and group homes. Her cutting became so severe that she received stitches multiple times, and once needed 77 staples to close up the wounds in her arms. Doctors flooded her with medications for the various disorders they labeled her with: anorexia, bulimia, addiction, borderline personality disorder, anxiety disorder, obsessive compulsive disorder.

That's who I am, Nicky told herself, embracing the diagnoses as a means of self-identification. *There actually is something wrong with me.*

The thought gave momentary validation, but instead of getting better, she continued spiraling out of control. Kim lived in a constant state of fear that each day would be Nicky's last. When Nicky was home and in her bedroom, Kim and her husband would ask one another, "Who's going up to check on her?" There was never assurance that they would find her alive.

When taking her to a group home or therapy session, Nicky would run into her mom's house one last time and take a handful of pills in the bathroom, or throw up again. Not only was she completely unpredictable, but her arguments with her mom became violent, and her step-dad had to pull them apart after Nicky lunged at Kim in the kitchen. Christmas and other holidays were spent in psychiatric units, with the family bringing gifts and spending a few hours with her.

Sometimes Nicky would escape from a hospital or center, leaving Kim to drive around until she would find her, take her back to the hospital and spend all night with her—before going into work. Kim's health soon bottomed out, and she ended up in the ICU where doctors said her body was completely depleted.

Kim also discovered the painful reality that when your child is diagnosed with a mental illness, people want to assign blame: "Maybe it's because you got married again, or had more kids," some suggested.

If Nicky had cancer, people would rally around us with bake sales and walks to raise awareness, Kim thought. *But nobody comes around to listen to what we're going through. They think it's all our fault.*

At 18, while living in a group home, Nicky started attending community college. She had been sober for a year, and optimism was awakened in her heart. Then her math tutor raped her. She relapsed hard into substance abuse, cutting and purging, losing weight at a life-threatening pace. When she vomited blood at the group home, the state transported her to an eating disorder unit, then to an in-patient psychiatric ward for four months.

This is my destiny, Nicky concluded, *to live in hospitals and be a ward of the state. That's my future. And yet, I've always thought there was something more—that somehow this cycle would end.*

Her negative assessment seemed to be confirmed at the next group home, where her house-mates were mostly women 20 to 30 years older than her who could not live independently. Two more suicide attempts and persistent self-harm led to monthly hospital visits for Nicky. One day, while walking to a convenience store, she passed out in a snow bank and was found by a passer-by who called an ambulance—and saved her from freezing to death.

Cocaine was the next level of addiction, and Nicky began

sleeping with fellow addicts just for access to the drug. By now she had burned most every bridge in her family, and Kim was so afraid of her that when Nicky stayed the night, Kim locked all other bedroom doors so Nicky couldn't have access to anyone. Sometimes Kim woke up and found strangers in the home and had to draw a line of safety by telling Nicky to leave.

One day, after a violent fit of rage in her group home, Nicky was moved to a short-term shelter. But because she was 21, and tired of failing at treatment, Nicky signed herself out and moved into a friend's apartment. That friend was also using drugs, and deeper darkness began to consume them both. To pay for her addiction, Nicky stole anything she could find, including her grandmother's jewelry, her older sister's credit card, and cash from wallets and purses that her relatives left in the spare bedroom during the family Christmas party.

At department stores, Nicky brazenly loaded up a cart with whatever she needed and simply walked out. She rarely got caught, but the shoplifting would eventually catch up to her.

I'm entitled to this because of the way the world has treated me, she thought to herself.

Even stealing wasn't enough to keep up with the insatiable need for cash for drugs. Her roommate used an internet site to find random men to sleep with for money. Nicky started doing the same and built a clientele. Days were spent waiting for "business" to come in through the website, or from walking the streets. None of it mattered to her. Addiction had narrowed her life to one question: How can I get the next high? What happened along the way seemed quickly forgotten.

Down to 100 pounds because of her eating disorder, Nicky found herself in increasingly dangerous situations, with strange men twice her age and twice her size, and in crack houses where she offered sex for drugs. State social workers continued coming to the apartment to provide medication and rides to therapy, none of which made much of a difference. Every moment of Nicky's life felt like trauma, and temporary relief only seemed to come from more drugs.

Kim, who was still in sporadic contact with Nicky, had prayed for many years that God would rescue her daughter. Now she prayed that Nicky would die.

What's the point of living if she's going to prostitute herself, put herself in danger and use drugs? she cried through tears of heartache. *If she is always going to be this miserable, why bother? God, just take her. She hates being alive, has no love, no joy, sees no future. This is no life at all. Please, let her die.*

Any phone call from Nicky brought overwhelming feelings of dread. Family and friends no longer wanted to hear about her because there was little they could say in the face of such extreme circumstances. Nicky's behavior had drained the family of peace and financial strength, and even caused Kim to turn down a major promotion at work because of Nicky's ongoing crisis.

Where does this end? Kim prayed. *There's no way to chart the future on this. God, our lives are being consumed by evil, by madness. It's beyond our control. There must be some way You can help.*

Nicky's grandmother had heard of Mercy Multiplied and urged Nicky to consider applying. After another suicide attempt, Nicky woke up in the hospital to see her mother's face.

"What about that program your grandmother has been talking about?" Kim said. "Do you want to give that a shot?"

Nicky thought, *I'm hooked on heroin, prostituting myself, stealing from family, and I just got arrested for shoplifting after a department store built a case against me. What other option do I have? I'm going to die otherwise. I've been in the finest hospitals in the United States here in Boston, and some of the top treatment centers. Yet nothing is working.*

While recovering in the psychiatric unit—her 43rd treatment facility—Nicky had access to a computer and completed step one and her first phone interview to apply to Mercy Multiplied. Her social worker included it in her treatment plan and did much of the legwork, getting medical records and signatures, and keeping Nicky moving forward.

But the worst was still ahead.

One day after being released from the psych unit, Nicky came back to the apartment to find her roommate with two guys she had just met.

"They want to pimp us out," the roommate said, as if this was a good thing.

The lead guy presented an arrangement in business terms.

"We can make it so you always have clients," he said. "And we have access to an unlimited supply of drugs."

This is not a good idea, Nicky thought, though the prospect of guaranteed payment was appealing since she'd had a number of guys skip out without paying. But the situation seemed out of her control. Now that the guys were in their apartment, there was nowhere else for her to go. And she was still addicted to heroin.

"The first thing that happens is I'm going to take you in that bathroom and break you," the lead guy told Nicky. What followed was the most violent rape she had experienced, a sick form of initiation and ownership.

The men then drove Nicky and her roommate to Providence, Rhode Island, and forced Nicky, who was older than her roommate, to go into a strip club to solicit customers. She returned with two guys who accompanied them to a nearby hotel room. If Nicky had failed to find clients, her new pimps made it clear they would have beaten her.

The pimps gave the girls heroin, and Nicky accidentally shot the drug into her muscle, one of the most painful experiences of her life. To make it worse, she was away from home and off all prescribed medications, and felt out of her mind. In the morning, after a hellish night of pain and debauchery, she called her therapist and asked to be rescued. The pimps, seeing Nicky as a sudden liability, dropped her off at her apartment. A social worker transported her to a detox hospital.

But when Nicky got out, she went straight back to using.

Please, God, she prayed, *if I don't get into Mercy, I don't know what will happen. This is the end for me.*

That week, a call came from Mercy Multiplied.

"You've been accepted into the program," the staff member said. "Here's the date you can come."

Kim immediately booked Nicky a ticket to Nashville. Relieved, Nicky still felt doubtful that anyone could handle a case like hers. She had been diagnosed with so many disorders, was on 14 prescribed medications, and had been told her situation was hopeless. Yet somehow she felt deep in her heart that one day she would get better. She just had no idea what that path looked like.

A few days before heading to the home in Nashville, she sat reading Mercy Multiplied books on her parents' back porch, while smoking marijuana. Suddenly, a strong, evil presence overshadowed her, filling her with terror and panic.

Oh, my gosh, what have I gotten myself into? she asked. *I can't go to Mercy Multiplied. This is not the place for me.*

Nicky had no experience with church outside of her nominally Catholic upbringing. Now a menacing voice spoke clearly to her mind.

Don't go, it said. *You don't belong there. It's the wrong place for you. Everything will get worse if you do.*

Nicky's breath came in short bursts, her lungs constricted with fear.

I must be hallucinating, she thought. *I'm hearing voices.*

Overcome by a sense of evil, she got up and went inside to look up Mercy Multiplied on the internet. Her search brought up a photo of smiling girls and young women who looked normal, even joyful. The darkness seemed to lessen as she stared at it.

"Okay, I think I'm going to be fine," Nicky told herself, still battling fear. "They're people like me. It'll be okay."

The spiritual struggle continued for two hours, and Nicky processed her thoughts in her journal, writing out a game plan: "I want to get sober. This is a residential center for drugs, eating disorders and cutting, and I've never been to a place that deals with all three. I'll be there for at least six months, sober, eating three meals a day, I won't be able to hurt myself or starve myself, and it's free of charge to me and my parents. Even if I don't like the God aspect, this will give me a little bit of stability. It will get me away from where I am now. If it doesn't work out, I can run away and start over and at least I'll be somewhere new."

Upon arriving at the Mercy Multiplied home in Nashville, Nicky briefly considered the possibility of procuring cigarettes and drugs while there, but kept pushing it back another week, knowing she'd be discharged from the program and could lose perhaps her last opportunity at life.

The girls' first big outing after Nicky arrived was to go water skiing. At the end of the day every girl received a medal with Jeremiah 29:11 on it, which read, "'For I know the plans I have for you,' declares the Lord, 'plans to prosper you and not to harm you, plans to give you hope and a future.'"

"This is such a great verse," the other girls said to each other. "I love it so much."

It's just words, Nicky thought skeptically. *I don't get it. It doesn't mean anything.*

But the girls and the staff had something she wanted—contentment, a sense of self, an ability to love. Nicky was especially intrigued by their conversations about the love of God. She didn't know such a thing existed.

She took the medal back to her room, looked at it for awhile and prayed, "God, I know this is supposed to mean something to me, but it doesn't. Help it mean something to me."

Nicky also committed to pray for ten minutes before bed every night, just to try it out. It didn't take long for the meaning and purpose in Jeremiah 29:11 to become deeply personal to her.

I see now, she thought after a few weeks of pondering the verse. *For the first time in my life, I feel like I have a choice to be free. All the treatment up to now was aimed at medicating and managing my problems, and they told me that mental illness and addiction were life sentences. But this verse, and everything at this place, tells me I can choose to live life, and that God has a purpose for me. I knew I had a future. Finally, Someone is agreeing with me!*

Six weeks into her stay at Mercy Multiplied, at a Wednesday evening church service, the pastor invited people to come forward to give their lives to Christ.

I think I want to go down there, Nicky thought, and slipped out of her row to walk to the front. She saw no fireworks and didn't feel much of anything, but prayed the prayer of salvation and went back to the home feeling good about her decision.

That week it occurred to Nicky that most of the clothing she brought with her to Mercy Multiplied, she had stolen from department stores.

You know, you can't just take whatever you want like you used to, she told herself. *The world doesn't owe it to you. These stolen clothes are holding you back somehow.*

She gathered up all her clothing and brought it to a staff member.

"I stole this stuff and I want to get rid of it," Nicky said. "I'll grab some clothes from the donation closet here."

That left her with just a few small items and some unused clothes from the donation closet.

This feels really good, she thought, reflecting on her decision later that day. *I want nothing from my former life. God, I want You to clothe me instead.*

Her attitude changed along with her wardrobe and her decision to follow Christ. Nicky had been aggressive, verbally threatening and prone to outbursts. She truly believed that the only emotion she was capable of was anger. Now when other girls expressed their pain, Nicky no longer became annoyed, but sympathized with their feelings. Decreasing anger was an answer to one of her specific, nightly prayers.

Some healing felt harder. The flashbacks, PTSD and nightmares were so strong that Nicky needed a staff member to pray with her at night before she went to bed.

I didn't know that stuff had affected my mind so much, Nicky thought, rattled by the severity of the memories. Even common household odors would set her off because some household substances are used in the preparation of drugs.

A terrifying flashback one day drove her to a staff member's office where Nicky sat on the floor, put her head on the staff member's knee and sobbed while the staff member prayed over her. Then Nicky saw something in her own mind—a scene of herself in a room at a crack house she use to frequent. But this time the Lord was there, too. He picked her up, carried her in His arms out of the room and far away from that place. The vision of them walking, she in His arms, lasted a long time and deeply healed part of Nicky's soul.

When Kim visited a couple of months into Nicky's stay at Mercy, she could hardly believe the change.

This is astounding, Kim thought, watching Nicky as they toured the home together. *Her "harsh" look is gone. She looks younger, and at rest. I'm starting to think this was a great choice.*

Kim could hardly be blamed for wondering if any change would be lasting, given how many other hospitals, centers and homes Nicky had burned through. On their last night together, they stood on the back porch.

"I'm really proud of you, Nicky," Kim said. She was not normally this expressive, and a lump formed in Nicky's throat as she took in the words. "I feel like I have my daughter back. For the first time in a really long time I am connecting with who you are, not just your mental illness and addiction."

They embraced, and that, too, healed inner wounds Nicky didn't even realize she had.

Other scars were more visible, like the abscessed ones on her arms from shooting heroin. Just glimpsing at her own veins triggered flashbacks and a rush of feelings and physical symptoms associated with using drugs. Praying with her counselor over this specific problem, Nicky saw a clear picture of herself in a garden sitting under a tree. The scene was beautiful and calm. Then Jesus came over to her and put an IV in her arm—and gave her a transfusion of His own blood. From that day forward Nicky experienced no PTSD episodes related to her past drug use.

Soon, the staff was treating Nicky like a leader among the girls, asking her to pray in group settings and lead by example. But when she was given her graduation date—February 7, 2013—Nicky cried for two days.

"I don't want to leave!" she yelled. "I have never felt this free and amazing. I still have a lot to deal with. And I'm scared of the future."

Her mini-tantrum didn't change their minds, so Nicky ran upstairs to her bedroom to pout. A little later, while grudgingly washing up for dinner, the numbers of her graduation date floated through her mind: 2 + 7 + 13 = 22. Nicky shot up from the sink and ran down the hall shouting, "Oh my gosh! God chose my graduation date!"

The number 22 had become very significant to her during her time at Mercy Multiplied. Nicky was 22 years old, and whenever she saw the number 22, she felt special, as if God was smiling at her. The other girls knew it and pointed it out whenever a 22 popped up. Flooded with confidence, she knew the graduation day had been given to her as a gift. Not only that, but one of her best friends in the home was graduating the same day. Nicky's entire family flew to Nashville to celebrate.

Nicky chose to stay in Nashville, with the support of her parents, and soon was coaching gymnastics, serving as a youth leader at her church, and traveling overseas on mission trips to places like Africa and China. She diligently kept the same habits of prayer and devotional time she had learned at Mercy Multiplied. Five years to the day after moving to Nashville, she moved back to Boston to attend Gordon College. She will graduate in May of 2019 with a degree in social work.

Returning to New England also offered the opportunity for deeper mending of family relationships which had already been much restored. One time, while helping her sister with her newborn baby for the summer, Nicky's sister told her, "I remember telling you I wanted you out of my life, that I would never trust you again, that I wanted no relationship with you. Now, if I died, you're the one I would want to raise my son."

Kim knew she had witnessed a miracle in Nicky's restoration.

"I didn't think you would survive," she told her daughter. "Without God and Mercy Multiplied, you wouldn't have."

The two spent many hours talking over and healing the past. At home and in her own career, Kim noticed herself becoming more sympathetic, slower to judge others for life problems, and more courageous about sharing her family's journey. She discovered that everyone struggles in some way and talking about it openly can help others.

Kim was promoted to vice president at her multi-national company, and the grace her boss extended during Nicky's time of crisis became the grace Kim shows to the 100 employees who now work under her leadership at a manufacturing facility. Kim was greatly impacted by the change in her daughter's life, and she came forward to commit her life to Christ at Mercy's Freedom Experience event in 2015. In her bathroom at home is a sign that reads, "'For I know the plans I have for you,' declares the Lord, 'plans to prosper you and not to harm you, plans to give you hope and a future.'—Jeremiah 29:11."

In addition to attending Gordon College, Nicky is working in a residential center as a Recovery Coach, coaching gymnastics, and speaks frequently at a halfway house in the area, sharing her powerful testimony and imparting hope to the women there. Upon graduation, Nicky plans to attend graduate school. She also wants to write a book about her life and someday open a residential home like Mercy Multiplied in New England.

———————————

Nicky's story is undoubtedly one of the most incredible stories of transformation that I have ever witnessed. The overwhelming emotions that came with the childhood abuse and her parents' divorce were more than Nicky felt she could handle. As a result, Nicky tried almost every possible coping mechanism for her pain—from an eating disorder to self-harm to alcohol to drugs to sex. She struggled with innumerable addictions.

Some people look at those struggling with an addiction—whether it's drugs, alcohol, pornography, or others—and don't understand why they just can't choose to stop. They don't understand that living with an addiction is like walking around every day with an iron ball and chain shackled to your leg. It goes with you everywhere. Every thought, action, and emotion can be affected by the addiction.

There are many root issues that can drive addiction, but one of the most common is abuse. Just as we see in Nicky's story, whether it is physical, sexual, verbal or emotional abuse, the overwhelming emotions abuse produces lead a person to find a way to escape the shame, pain, guilt, and anger. These intense emotions can leave a huge void inside their heart. They may have reached for the first thing available as a temporary "fix", but before they know it, that fix has become a normal part of their daily life from which they cannot seem to break free.

If you are struggling with an addiction, you may believe that you have no choice, but you do. You may think that the addiction has ultimate power over your life, but I promise you there is a power that's greater. Nothing on this earth will ever be able to fill the void in your life that only Jesus Christ can fill. There's not a sufficient amount of any substance that will bring you the emotional fulfillment your heart is desperate for. In fact, relying on anything besides God to ease your pain will have the opposite effect: You'll be left feeling more hopeless than ever before. Only God can heal the pain and release you from the need to turn to those addictive behaviors.

When Nicky came to Mercy, she learned how to take the pain of her past to Jesus. In her story, she shared about a powerful moment in counseling when she was taken back to a memory of herself in a room at a crack house she used to frequent, but this time the Lord was there, and He picked her up and carried her out of the room. That vision deeply healed part of Nicky's soul.

Every one of us experiences hurt, but when those hurts remain unhealed, we walk around with limps. The enemy wants to use our hurts to hold us in bondage. Freedom means no longer allowing hurts to direct our lives and destroy our relationships. Many people don't want to acknowledge their hurts because of the painful emotions attached to them. Instead of running to God, they run away from Him. But your unhealed hurts will always catch up with you. The only safe place to run is to Him.

As we see in Nicky's story, pouring out our emotions to God is where inner healing begins. Being open and honest with Him is vital in helping us move forward. He is not afraid or offended by our anger, our disappointment, or our confusion, even if it is directed at Him.

The good news is that God has a response to our pain, anger, and disappointment. He has something to say about the painful situations we have faced, and He wants to bring healing and show us His perspective. He was never the source of our pain, but He will be the source for our healing if we allow Him to be. Isaiah 53:5 says that we are healed by His wounds, and Psalm 147:3 says, "He heals the brokenhearted and binds up their wounds." Allowing the Holy Spirit to speak into the hurtful and painful experiences of our lives is a vitally important key to freedom. However, you may want to consider doing this with a Christian counselor, pastor, or mentor if you feel it's appropriate for your situation (i.e. when the memories of the past are particularly traumatic).

Prior to coming to Mercy, Nicky had been diagnosed as an addict, bipolar, as having borderline personality disorder, anxiety disorder and obsessive-compulsive disorder. Sadly, as many do, she had taken these diagnoses on as her identity. She had been in over 42 different treatment facilities, hospitalized over a hundred times, and was on 14 prescribed medications when she walked through our doors. She was convinced that her destiny was to live in hospitals. The world clearly did not have an answer for Nicky.

Anyone looking at Nicky's situation would have been tempted to say that there was no hope for her. Her own mother prayed that she would die, because she never thought Nicky would get out of the situation she was in. It just reminds me of what Jesus said in Luke 18:27: "What is impossible with man is possible with God." If I have learned anything throughout my years at Mercy, it is that *nothing* is too hard for God. No life is too far gone. There is no such thing as a life that cannot be changed.

While at Mercy, the power of Jesus' death and resurrection became real to Nicky. The truth of God's Word began to expose and uproot the lies she had believed. The love of Christ began to heal what was broken in Nicky's heart. Her identity in Christ overcame the identity of her innumerable diagnoses. Through the promise of Jeremiah 29:11, Nicky was able to replace the belief that she was destined to live in hospitals with the belief that God has an amazing future planned for her. Through the Holy Spirit, she was able to receive from God what no treatment program or medication could provide for her.

I love how the radical transformation in Nicky's life so powerfully impacted the life of her mother. I can only imagine the desperation Kim must have felt as she watched her daughter's life spinning out of control. And although she had not committed her life to Christ when Nicky entered the Mercy program, Kim saw what seemed to be a hopeless situation miraculously turn around. She could not deny the power of Christ when she looked at her daughter, and eventually made the decision to commit her own life to Him. In the end, Kim couldn't argue with Nicky's changed life, and surely no one else can!

reason
EIGHT

Kirsten

Kirstin enjoyed life in suburban New Jersey with two sisters and parents who never seemed to fight. Then, during Christmas vacation when she was 13, her parents sat her and her younger sisters down.

"We have some big news for you," their mother said. "We are getting divorced."

Kirstin's jaw dropped. Her sisters were just as shocked. None of them had seen this coming.

"The four of us are moving to Florida," their mother continued. "Your dad is staying in New Jersey."

Four days later, the three girls and their mother were in a moving truck heading south. They enrolled in a private school and tried to settle in for the second half of the school year.

What just happened to my life? Kirstin wondered, while looking at the dark ceiling in her new bedroom. *Everything's new—new house, new family dynamics, new school, no friends. I have so few answers. Why didn't I see this coming?*

Struggling to fit in at school, Kirstin came home each day, sat on the couch and watched TV. Gone was the active lifestyle she'd had in New Jersey. A couple of months later, their dad visited for the first time.

"Oh, I see you've put on some weight," he said to Kirstin.

Huh? Kirstin thought. She hadn't even thought of her weight before that moment.

"If you want to lose it, I'd be happy to help you," he offered. "I could give you some tips to lose it really fast. Just let me know."

Obsession with dieting was common in her father's family—she knew that much. Kirstin had never seen her grandmother eat a meal—she only picked at things. Her father would starve himself, then binge-eat. So would several of his sisters and their children. To Kirstin, it was normal because it was the family culture. One night, when she was younger, she had even witnessed her dad binge. Kirstin had fallen asleep on the couch watching a movie and was awakened in the middle of the night by the fridge light. She spied her dad eating a whole pound of sliced ham.

That's weird, she thought and went back to sleep.

The next day her mom was making sandwiches for a jaunt to the beach.

"Where's all the ham?" she asked. "I just bought it yesterday."

"Kirstin ate it," her dad replied.

"I did not!" she burst out.

Why would he lie and say I ate it? she thought. *That's bizarre.*

Now, in Florida, she concluded she had gained weight since the move, mostly from being friendless and depressed.

"I'm ready to lose some weight," Kirstin told her dad before he left. "Tell me what to do."

He proceeded to share in detail about what fats, carbs and other things were, counting calories, keeping a food diary, and weighing yourself daily to keep track of your progress. Days later, he mailed her a workout video.

It worked: Kirstin lost weight quickly, and became physically fit again. Kids at her school took notice.

"Hey, you look good. How did you lose the weight so fast?" girls inquired. Popular people invited her to sit at their lunch tables.

I haven't had this much attention since we moved, Kirstin thought. *Gotta say, it feels pretty good.*

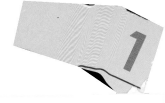

For six months, she lived a healthy lifestyle, working out every other day and weighing herself once daily. But her new friends were more enthusiastic dieters, sharing tips every day over lunch. They even wrapped themselves in cellophane and sat in a hot tub to sweat out water weight.

For them, it seemed to mostly be youthful excess, but for Kirstin, it began consuming her thoughts. She suddenly felt the need to control every aspect of her eating and appearance, so she cut out breakfast, then lunch, and began weighing herself several times a day. Within six months some girls at her school who had eating disorders were in a competition to be thinnest. They swapped low-calorie food ideas, held each other accountable to work out three times a day (before school, after school and in the locker room before lunch) and lied to cover up for each other.

At the same time, Kirstin was becoming involved at her church youth group, mentoring younger girls, leading Sunday school and eventually being chosen to serve as president of the youth group. It was the essence of a double life. At school, she obsessed over popularity and her weight, while at church she prayed and spoke into other girls' lives.

This went on for five years, until the summer she was 17, when a Lifetime movie brought the truth home. In it, a girl who played high school volleyball developed an eating disorder. Kirstin was astounded to see that the girl's behaviors were almost identical to her own.

Wait a second, she thought. *I do the same things that girl is doing! What?!*

That Friday night at youth group she told her youth pastor she thought she had an eating disorder, and together they told her mom. They agreed to meet for regular counseling, but the counselor was ill-equipped to handle Kirstin's issues. The only eating disorders he'd heard of were in Hollywood, and his main advice was, "You have to just start eating."

"I can't," Kirstin said.

"You have to," he repeated.

This isn't working, Kirstin thought. At one point, another pastor brought in a hamburger.

"You have to eat this," he said.

"I'm not eating that," Kirstin said. They looked at her in frustration.

While Kirstin appreciated their efforts and loved them at the same time, she knew that the problem was deeper than her just not eating. Deep-seated heart issues were involved. As much as she made plans and set goals to eat more, she couldn't bring herself to do it.

At the end of her senior year, her friends were excited to head off to college, but Kirstin knew that if she left home she would spin out of control.

I've got a really big issue, she thought, *and I know that eating disorders are way worse at college. I can't go.*

Unable to see anything beyond her bondage, and unable to afford the secular treatment programs she and her mom researched, Kirstin felt stuck without a future. Then her mom heard about Mercy Multiplied and the lives of the young women who had been transformed there on Joyce Meyer's television program.

"Oh, my gosh, Kirstin. This is it!" she yelled.

Over the next few months, Kirstin began filling out the Mercy Multiplied application five different times—and threw each one away. One completed application even ended up on the highway.

I don't want to go! she screamed in her own head, tossing the application out the window while driving 65 miles per hour. *I want to live my life, not go away and work on this stupid problem. I don't want people to make me gain weight! I'm not going.*

Within weeks or even days it was clear she was slipping further into the abyss. Finally, she mailed in an application and received a call from a Mercy staff member in the Intake Department: "There's a bed open in Monroe, Louisiana. If you're ready, you can come here."

On the short airplane ride, Kirstin committed to try a different path: *I'm giving this everything I've got. No shortcuts, no lying. Do it right—give it your all.*

She walked into an atmosphere of love when she stepped through the doors of the Monroe home.

This feels like a home, not a treatment center, she thought. *There's so much love coming from the staff and the girls. This is nothing like I pictured.*

When they asked if she wanted to start on minimal meal requirements, which is initially an option for young women with eating disorders, Kirstin said no. That became a defining moment. She immersed herself in everything—worship, relationships, reading and researching. The intensity of the work matched her intensity to change. As she watched herself transform from the inside out, she was encouraged to embrace the program even more.

Everything except the truth statements.

This is ridiculous, she told herself. *I'm not going to do it. I'll look like an idiot saying this stuff out loud.*

She finally decided to give it a try, but she began in a whisper.

"Kirstin is beautifully and wonderfully made."

That wasn't so bad.

"Kirstin is a daughter of the King."

Okay. I guess.

She could hear other residents outside speaking their truth statements out loud with authority.

This is crazy, she thought again, but continued whispering her statements.

Over the weeks, her whisper grew to full voice as a new kind of confidence emerged.

This is literally changing my thought process, how I see the world, how I understand God and how He feels about me, she realized one day. *It's like new pathways in my brain are being created. When you walk down a path many times, you crush the grass down and it becomes easy to go that way again. Now I feel the grass growing on the old, bad pathways that I'm leaving behind, and the new pathways feel more natural.*

Counseling proved a powerful tool as well. Kirstin had never been in professional counseling or gotten to the root issue of her disorder: control. Now she was given tools to handle old temptations.

Still, graduation day seemed to come too early. She walked into her counselor's office that morning.

"I don't think I'm ready," Kirstin announced.

"What do you mean?" the counselor asked.

"I feel like I still struggle a little bit," Kirstin confessed. "I still have to fight temptations."

"Temptation may regularly be there, but now you have the tools," the counselor replied. "You know exactly what to do and how to not act on those behaviors. You can do this."

Kirstin sighed. *They've been right about everything else,* she thought.

"Okay," she said. That day she gave a beautiful testimony in front of the entire house and all the guests.

After graduating from Mercy in 2006, Kirstin knew she wanted to spend her life empowering women somehow, and she chose the direction of counseling. Southeastern University, a Christian school in Florida, seemed the perfect place to start life again.

I'm going to focus on my schoolwork, Kirstin promised herself. *No dating, no nothing. I'm doing this right.*

But in an English Composition 1 class that fall, she met Tomas. Tomas had rolled up to campus from Key West in his Volkswagen Passat with a surfboard on the roof and hair down to his shoulders. He had grown up in the Czech Republic. His parents had been house church members and Bible smugglers under Communist rule—hard-working people and prayer warriors who stood on the Word of God. It was not until the Berlin Wall came down, they were able to openly take their kids to church, Sunday school and youth group.

When Tomas was ten, his family won the green card lottery, and they moved from a little town in the middle of nowhere in Eastern Europe to the southernmost point of the United States. The only English he knew, he told people half-jokingly, was "Coca-Cola" and "Hallelujah."

In Key West they joined an Assembly of God church and his dad began serving as the worship pastor there, in addition to building a well-respected tile, remodeling and construction business.

Strongly impressed by his parents' commitment to overseas

missions, especially to Haiti, Tomas came into Southeastern University as a Missions major.

That guy's super chill, Kirstin observed as they edited each other's papers. *And he's funny and loves God. But I'm not here to date, I'm here to learn.*

One day she drove by a lake and saw Tomas journaling on the shore.

Wow, that's really attractive, she couldn't help thinking. So she called her mom.

"You know that list I made when I got home from Mercy—the top ten things I want in my future husband?" she said. "Get it out and read it to me."

All ten of her requirements seemed to fit Tomas, and the more she prayed about it, the more peace she felt. They started dating and immediately felt comfortable together.

Five months later, Tomas took her home to meet his parents in Key West, and a friend flew them around the island in a Cessna airplane. Tomas and his father had written in large letters, using drywall compound, on an old bridge, "Kirstin, I love you. Marry me."

Looking down, Kirstin said, "Oh, my gosh, look. Someone has my name."

The ring convinced her the invitation was for her. A year later, in 2009, they were married in Homosassa, Florida, at a garden on the water. They moved into a house in Lakeland and attended school while both working. Balancing new married life, school and jobs posed a challenge to the young couple, but they were determined to make it work and fulfill their numerous responsibilities.

Kirstin and Tomas finished their undergraduate degrees, and then went on to get their master's degrees together.

But becoming a therapist did not seem to be the right fit for Kirstin. She had discovered how good healthy, balanced exercise and clean eating could make her feel. She redirected her efforts and went to nutrition school for a year and also earned fitness certifications. When she looked for work at a place that helped women in a holistic way, she found nothing.

"It sounds like there's a real need for what you're wanting," Tomas said. "Why don't you start it?"

"Me? Start a business?" she asked.

"Yeah," he replied. "A business is finding a need and filling a need."

Maybe I could do something like that, she considered.

As soon as she began planning, God seemed to provide everything as confirmation: a rent-free studio, free advertising, and a team of fitness instructors enthusiastic to help start the studio. Their goal: to empower women and help them be the best versions of themselves.

Kirstin began blogging to share the process of starting the business, including her apprehensions, hurdles, and things God was doing, along with her passion for nutrition and fitness. She also shared about her past eating disorder and Mercy Multiplied's impact on her life. By the time the studio opened, Kirstin had a significant local following. Within seven months her studio took over the office next door and tripled their space.

Meanwhile, Tomas had discovered his business acumen and pioneered a financial planning and insurance brokerage firm from scratch, growing it to 90 employees before he turned 30 years of age. He and Kirstin adopted two children as their preferred way of starting a family. They are involved at Grace City Church in Lakeland, Florida, where Kirstin's best friend is one of the pastors.

In 2016, ten years after graduating the program, the leadership at Mercy invited Kirstin to come to the Nashville location to speak to the residents, share her story, and encourage them. The experience was "surreal and incredible," she said afterward. "There were many emotional moments for me to see God's work full-circle in my life. Being back at Mercy reminded me even more of the ripple effect that has taken place since I graduated from the program. My life mission is to empower women because of the work God did in me at Mercy. I know that it is my calling to 'pay this forward.' Being back at Mercy once again fueled that passion to another level!"

Today, Kirstin's studio is a first-class operation run by a team of forty women, offering up to a dozen classes a day in Pilates, yoga, kick boxing, boot camp and more, and enjoying a huge presence in their community. The program is called Balance Culture, and everything they do is done with excellence.

One day a woman reached out Kirstin, because she had heard that Kirstin had once struggled with an eating disorder and now had a nutrition practice at her studio. This woman shared about her daughter, Megan's, struggle with an eating disorder. Kirstin met with Megan, and soon after, Megan joined the Balance Culture community and started taking fitness classes at the studio.

About a month later, though, it became clear to Kirstin that Megan needed more help than Kirstin could offer, so she shared with Megan about how God radically transformed her life during her time at Mercy Multiplied. Kirstin was so proud of Megan as she bravely made moves toward the Mercy program and eventually submitted her application. Megan entered the doors of Mercy in the spring of 2018. She and Kirstin have kept in touch while Megan has been in the program.

"It has been amazing to hear Megan talk about how her relationship with God is growing and to hear how God is moving in her life," Kirstin says. "Satan took fitness and nutrition and tried to destroy me with it. God turned it around and now uses those things in my life to empower women. That's a huge testament to who God is. Mercy was that turning point for me. The biggest blessing for me is helping women feel like the best versions of themselves, and to have a role in their lives the way Mercy had in mine, and hopefully to be used by God in the same way."

———————————

Eating disorders are devastating millions of lives across the world, affecting mostly females, but sometimes males, too. Many cases go unreported as people struggle in silence and secrecy. How does the seemingly insignificant desire to lose a few pounds become something so powerful that it demands control of your entire life? Many people like Kirstin surpass their goal to lose a few pounds and progress into an overwhelming addiction, a coping mechanism to deal with their own pain.

For Kirstin, much of that pain came from her parents' divorce and the struggle with fitting in at a new school. If you remember from her story, it only took one comment from her father about her weight to open the door to what would become a serious life-controlling issue. As Kirstin began losing weight and popular kids at school started noticing her and including her, her obsession was fueled.

While at Mercy, Kirstin learned the root issue underneath her eating disorder: control. This is a very common root issue for people who struggle with eating disorders. Interestingly, while the behaviors associated with an eating disorder make you feel like you are in control, the very opposite is true. When you choose to give in to the harmful behaviors of anorexia, bulimia, or binge-eating, you are actually giving control of your life and your thoughts to your enemy, the devil. The Bible tells us in 2 Peter 2:19 that we are slaves to whatever controls us. The way to walk in freedom is to choose to surrender control of your life to God instead of trying to control your life yourself.

I find it so interesting that one of the most vital keys to freedom for Kirstin was initially one of the hardest for her. While at Mercy, she was at first very resistant to the whole idea of renewing her mind. But as she, slowly but surely, started replacing the lies that had fed her behaviors, she learned that renewing her mind was going to be an ongoing process, not a one-time event.

In *Keys to Freedom*, we talk about how our thought patterns are like hiking trails. Creating a new hiking trail requires some short-term effort of removing trees and creating a tread surface. But trails are maintained by people regularly walking on them, right? The more a trail is walked on, the more established it becomes. On the other hand, if people stop walking on the trail, it will eventually disappear.

Our "thought trails" have been well used over the years and many of them developed from a young age. The only way to re-direct our thoughts is to stop walking down the old thought trails and choose to create new ones. Rather than always replaying the lies, you can introduce new *true* thoughts into your mind.

Breaking down the old well-worn trails of thought doesn't happen involuntarily. It requires a daily choice. However, if you have begun the process of renewing your mind and still find those old lies creeping in, don't give up! As you commit to the process, over time, the new thoughts based on the truth of God's Word will actually become more natural in your mind than the old faulty beliefs.

One of my favorite parts of Kirstin's story is how her choice to pursue freedom literally put an end to a generational pattern that had been passed on to her. We learn from her story that obsession with dieting was common in her father's family. She had never seen her grandmother eat a meal, and her father, along with several of his sisters and their children, would starve themselves, then binge-eat.

To Kirstin, this behavior was completely normal. It was part of the family culture in which she had been raised. That's the problem with generational patterns: we often assume that what we see and experience as children is "normal." You can't imagine how many people I have met who were abused as children, but assumed that abuse was a normal thing. As a result, we often mindlessly follow suit and become what has been modeled to us.

However, as Kirstin realized the destruction of her choices and the bondage in which she was living, she chose a new way. She chose to stand in her authority as a daughter of God and put an end to the life-controlling issue that had so infiltrated her biological family. She was able to establish new patterns that are now bringing blessing to her future, her children's futures, and to the futures of all those she influences.

The enemy sought to destroy Kirstin's life through an eating disorder, and she is not only free of that issue, she is helping other women find freedom from the same struggles! Her desire through her business is to help women not only with their own emotional needs, but fitness and nutrition as well. I love how awesome our God is that He is able to take the very thing that the enemy tried to use to destroy us, and it ends up being the thing used to destroy him!

I am so impressed by what Kirstin is doing through her business, The Balance Culture. It is a state-of-the-art facility that is clearly run with the highest levels of excellence. We have asked Kirstin to come and speak with our residents at our Nashville location a couple of times since she graduated—once in 2016 and again in 2018. Kirstin spends two days with us when she comes: she shares her testimony with the residents, then eats lunch and goes to recreation with them. On the second day, she teaches the residents about mindful eating, healthy dietary guidelines, and how to create a diet that is based on moderation. It is always so powerful to hear Kirstin share how her own struggle led her to become passionate about healthy, clean eating, and built the foundation for her business.

When Kirstin was with us in 2018, one resident shared afterwards, "I loved Kirstin! I was so impacted by the way she explained getting through the struggles she went through and how she got the help she needed. I know I will get through my own struggles, too." Another resident shared, "I loved this lesson because it was awesome to see how Kirstin's life has completely changed after Mercy. Her message filled me with hope that my life can transform like this, too."

What an incredible blessing to see the testimonies of

former Mercy residents encourage and inspire our current Mercy residents! But it doesn't stop there for Kirstin. She is one of Mercy's Graduate Ambassadors, which means that she has spoken at many different places to many different groups of people, sharing her story of transformation to men and women of all ages. Her story has impacted countless people—whether it be within the walls of one of our Mercy homes, within the walls of her fitness studio, or in the innumerable other places where God has used her testimony to fill others with hope and life!

reason

NINE

Amber & Sarah

Amber McCarter was a precocious, brilliantly artistic girl who enjoyed the mission field in Kenya where her parents, Kyle and Victoria, built a medical clinic. At three years old, she was so articulate and confident speaking in public that the African people thought she was an adult in a child's body. (They also thought she was blind because of her bright blue eyes.) When the McCarters moved back to their home state of Illinois, Amber's schoolmates dubbed her the attorney of the class because she argued and communicated so well.

Athletically built, and relatively new to town, Amber faced some verbal bullying in high school and struggled to make friends. Switching to a private school only raised the pressure because the other kids wore name brands that the McCarters couldn't afford while starting their own manufacturing business. When a kid at school criticized her new hair style, Amber came home and cut it all off.

Painting, sketching and drawing came effortlessly to her, as did anything academic. But her self-image sank lower as social acceptance eluded her. Her vibrant laugh, famous among family and friends, died down, and the happy girl her parents and brothers knew seemed to disappear behind a cloud of negative emotions.

One day she was invited to join a popular group of kids who wanted to go shoplifting. When they got caught, they told their parents it was Amber's fault. Nobody else was disciplined.

Hanging around boys instead of girls didn't help. One relationship turned serious and sexual, and the McCarters sent Amber to a private Christian boarding school in another state to remove her from the environment. The school turned out to be very legalistic, and Amber experienced the bitter taste of religion instead of a life-giving relationship with God.

Back home, after graduating from high school in 2004, she enrolled at cosmetology school and pursued her passion for fashion. Amber had a knack for putting together the right boots, skirts and accessories. By the time she was 20 years old, she was working part-time and going after her dream.

Out of nowhere, Kyle and Victoria began receiving threatening calls from credit card companies. They investigated and found that Amber had met a guy at work who was a major drug dealer in the area. He had gotten her addicted to heroin. Together, they were stealing from anywhere they could and using heroin in local flop houses.

Hearts broken, the McCarters found themselves in a nightmare as their daughter's life had hit rock-bottom, yet she was trying to hide it from them. But as arrests and calls from the county jail became common, so did her mother's fervent prayers.

"Lord, don't let her die tonight," Victoria said, staring at the darkness above her bed at night. "Please protect her no matter what she does."

Phone messages were seldom returned, but Victoria left them anyway: "Honey, I love you and God has a plan for your life. Please let us know how you are doing."

Kyle had been elected a county board member in 2000, so calls from the police were particularly awkward. But they also brought relief: the nights Amber spent at the county jail were the only nights Kyle and Victoria slept well because they knew their daughter would be alive in the morning.

One day, light seemed to shine through the darkness. Amber admitted she needed help and wanted to get clean. Kyle picked her up at the police station.

"Can we go to the house I was staying in to get my things?" she asked.

Kyle steered the car to a part of town where he didn't expect to find a dope house. The neighborhood was nice, but the residence was filthy, with foil wrappers, spoons and other drug waste everywhere, and obvious places on the floor and couches where people slept.

This is in the suburbs, not the ghetto, Kyle thought, amazed. *I had no idea drug culture was so close to normal life.*

Amber took her time fetching her things. They learned later that she had used once more while there that day, knowing she wouldn't be able to in the treatment center where she was headed.

30 days in the center seemed to work, getting Amber clean from the "demon" drug, as Kyle called it. But Kyle and Victoria knew she needed deeper life changes to maintain her victory. Victoria had heard about Mercy Multiplied at a Joyce Meyer conference and made it her goal for Amber to go there.

"Look at these girls," Victoria said, showing Amber the Mercy Multiplied magazine and website. "They are so joyful and free. This is the life we want for you. We want you to experience this same freedom."

Amber started the application process to Mercy in 2006. At the same time, drug dealers did everything they could to reach her. The McCarters disconnected her cell phone, her home phone and got her mail rerouted to their business office. While waiting for a spot to open up at Mercy, Amber stayed at a local rehabilitation clinic for a week because she was not strong enough to be left alone yet for any stretch of time.

When her parents came to check on her one day, she had signed herself out of the clinic.

"Where did she go?" Kyle asked the administrators.

"We don't know," they replied. "She said she wanted to leave."

"Didn't you try to stop her?"

"No, that's not our job," they said.

"Did she leave with anyone?" he pressed.

"Yes, with some people she met here," they said.

"Couldn't you have called us?" he asked.

"No, because she's not a minor," they replied.

This is not good, Victoria thought, trying to keep herself from imagining the worst.

Phone call after phone call turned up nothing. Nobody had seen Amber or heard from her. Two days later, the police called Kyle. Their voices sounded grim.

"We need to meet with you," the officer said.

Kyle was just leaving a county board meeting. He met the officers in a nearby parking lot.

"We found your daughter lying on the side of the railroad tracks, arms crossed, fully clothed," the officer said. "Someone put her there. It looks like she died of a drug overdose."

A thousand thoughts rushed through his mind. Among them was, *If only she had made it to Mercy. She was so close to freedom.*

The autopsy showed heroin laced with Fentanyl, a strong pain reliever normally given to cancer patients late in life. Amber died on June 24, 2006. She was 21 years old.

In the midst of their shock and grief, Kyle and Victoria called Mercy and asked them to set up an information table at Amber's funeral. In lieu of memorial gifts, they asked friends and family to give to Mercy Multiplied in memory of Amber. Since Mercy brings in young women free of charge,

God laid it on Kyle's heart to set a goal of raising $30,000 for Mercy to help girls like Amber. Kyle and Victoria wanted to use what the enemy meant for harm to produce life for someone else. They ended up exceeding their goal.

As it turned out, their relationship with Mercy Multiplied was just beginning. The St. Louis home dedicated a room to Amber and hung her artwork there. Then the McCarters began opening their personal home to Mercy graduates to offer them a stable place to live, work and find their footing after graduating.

One of those girls was Sarah. In her home state of Minnesota, Sarah had seemed to enjoy a normal small-town childhood, but she was being abused and trafficked for sex by a family acquaintance from an early age. Sarah saw money change hands, and drugs in the abuser's house, and feared telling anyone what was happening.

The abuse stopped after a couple of years, and Sarah tried to act like it had never happened. Born with a great sense of humor, she became the class clown, and other people's laughter became her wall of defense. Self-harm, alcohol, drugs, and an eating disorder were her numbing agents behind closed doors. In her senior year, she tried to take her life with pills.

Because she had just turned 18, she was sent to an adult mental hospital and found herself surrounded by schizophrenics and people screaming in the halls. But she began reading a book her friend gave her by the founder of Mercy Multiplied called *Mercy Moves Mountains*, and the testimonies deeply impressed her.

Wow, there are people out there who have gone through what I have! she thought. *Okay, I'll give it a try.*

She printed off the Mercy application while in the mental

hospital and mailed it in, promising her mother and her youth pastor's wife, "I'll give this program a try, and if I hate it and it doesn't work, I'm coming back."

Sarah entered the St. Louis Mercy home in June of 2007. Unconditional love from the staff, and the peace resting on the home, convinced her within moments that she belonged there. When Victoria McCarter visited the home, shared Amber's story and gave each girl a copy of a painting Amber had made, it greatly encouraged Sarah.

There have been times when I wondered, is it worth it to be here? Do I want to stick it out? she thought. *Hearing Amber's story makes me a lot more grateful. I'm getting the chance she never had.*

The Lord transformed Sarah's life during her time at Mercy, and when she graduated in December of 2007, she enrolled at Trinity Bible College in North Dakota. After her first semester there, was invited to spend the summer at the McCarters' house. Not only that, but Kyle gave her a summer job at their manufacturing facility where she and several other women sewed items for the athletic training market.

One time Sarah walked into his office and said almost nonchalantly, "I'm finished with what you gave me to do."

She can't be, Kyle thought.

"Didn't I give you four things?" he inquired gently.

"Yeah, I did 'em," she said in her understated way.

"Let's go take a look," he said, and walked with Sarah onto the factory floor. There on a table were the items she had sewn, exactly as he wanted them. He shook his head.

"Sarah, you're so fast and so smart that I think you could run this place," he said. Sarah grinned.

Church attendance, family meals and the basic rhythms

of life gave Sarah a much-needed education on healthy family life. She watched carefully that summer how Kyle and Victoria behaved as husband and wife, father and mother.

Wow. This is what I want my life to look like one day when I become a wife and a mother, she thought in her room one night after dinner. *These have to be two of the coolest people I've ever met. They're so generous, so ministry-minded, and they love on people so much. Between them and the Mercy home, I feel like I'm learning how to really live.*

After graduating from Trinity Bible College in 2011, Sarah reconnected with a guy she had met there named Jesse. He worked two hours away in a Teen Challenge center, while Sarah worked at a home in South Dakota for girls with behavioral issues. Uncharacteristically for her, Sarah asked him out on their first date.

"You did what?" her mother exclaimed when Sarah told her. "The last time we talked, you said you didn't even want to be married!"

Until then, Sarah had stuck with her plan to stay single and perhaps adopt a child alone. But Jesse had a number of the same positive qualities Sarah had observed in Kyle.

I think he might make a good husband and father, she thought.

Their first date, which was at a coffee shop located between their two towns, lasted for four hours as they shared about their passions, their jobs and what they wanted to do with their lives. After three months of long-distance dating, Jesse proposed. Six months after that, they were married.

Little did Sarah know that the people who'd been like second parents to her, and who she'd so admired, would be attending her wedding in 2012. Kyle and Victoria encouraged her yet again as she and Jesse pursued a call into youth ministry. After serving in several churches, Jesse was hired by Life Church in Oklahoma.

Today, Sarah spends much time with young people at the church and is drawn to hurting girls, especially those who self-harm. Sometimes her own scars open doors for deeper conversations with girls who are struggling.

Sarah and Jesse have two children and one on the way. "I wouldn't have this life, or any life at all, without the McCarters and Mercy Multiplied," she said. "They gave me the hope and the tools to live in freedom in Jesus. I couldn't be more grateful."

In February of 2009, Kyle was appointed to serve the remaining term for Illinois's 54th state senate district, then won the election three times after that. Their eldest son, Zach, attended the Air Force Academy and is now a Captain serving in the US Air Force. He has been happily married to his wife, Claire, for several years and is currently on assignment in Africa. Their younger son, Austin, and his wife, Catherine, are living in Illinois and are the proud parents of a daughter, Cora Lee. Austin is now the president of the McCarter family business, Custom Product Innovations.

Kyle used his decade in the state senate to promote pilot programs for heroin addicts in state prisons. When he stood to speak in the senate, the room typically went quiet because when he spoke about families and young people with addictions, it was with a hard-earned authority.

He also used his position to bring young women from the St. Louis Mercy home to the senate floor and introduce them as his heroes.

"The biggest shout-out I can give for Mercy is that these are programs that really work," he said. "Government is not the answer here. You can't throw money at a cultural problem and expect to fix it. But ministries like Mercy are showing how lifelong, lasting change can be accomplished."

The McCarters have generously housed 14 Mercy graduates over the years, and have hired many of them to work in their business. The McCarters' generosity has allowed many young women to have cars of their own and a jump start into a successful future.

In March of 2018, Kyle was appointed by President Trump to serve as the U.S. Ambassador to Kenya, and he is currently awaiting confirmation by the Senate. Kyle made sure that Mercy Multiplied was mentioned in the White House press release. They were blown away by the providence of God that Kyle would be appointed to the very country where they lived when Amber was born and had since visited multiple times for mission work.

As Kyle has told Mercy residents a number of times, "I wouldn't wish the tough parts of my story on anybody, but what the enemy meant for harm, we decided to let God use for good. We are going to win this battle and use our experience to save as many girls like Amber as possible. Mercy Multiplied's staff is empowered by God to help. That's what makes all the difference. That's why it's so successful."

Little did I know on June 24, 2006, when we first got the call about Amber dying of a drug overdose, that I would become such close personal friends with Kyle and Victoria and that they would remain in my life and in the lives of all of our St. Louis residents and staff. Our friendship continues to grow stronger with each passing day, and they have already invited me and our team to Kenya to visit them and do outreach there. They want us to bring our *Keys to Freedom* study so that it can spread throughout the nation of Kenya. We are very, very excited about all that God has in store for the future as a result of their position in Kenya and our relationship with them. This is yet another great example of what I believe will prove to be exponential multiplication of freedom in the nation of Kenya and beyond.

No one familiar with the way Amber McCarter died could blame her mom and dad for being angry and bitter. Yet, somehow Kyle and Victoria made a decision from the very onset that they would not allow themselves to become bitter, but rather they would choose to do exactly what Kyle said: "What the enemy meant for harm, we decided to let God use for good."

Since 2006, I have watched Kyle and Victoria love and support every young woman who walks through the doors of the St. Louis Mercy home. Sarah was one of the first. In fact, Sarah entered the St. Louis program in June 2007, exactly one year after Amber lost her battle to drug addiction.

When Sarah first arrived, Victoria came to the St. Louis home to tell her story about Amber. Sarah was greatly impacted, and immediately grateful that she was getting the opportunity Amber never had.

Sarah graduated six months later in December 2007, and the McCarters were there for her on her special day. The McCarters were like second parents to Sarah, and Sarah became like a second daughter to the McCarters.

After Mercy, Sarah completed her first semester of college in the first half of 2008, and the McCarters not only invited Sarah to spend the summer with them, they also offered to give her a summer job working in their manufacturing facility. She was very moved by their love and support, and as you can see from reading the story, they were there at every important time in her life. They were there for her wedding in 2012, and they have also been very encouraging to Sarah and Jesse as they pursue their call to youth ministry and are now on staff with Life Church in Oklahoma. To this day, the McCarters remain very influential in Sarah's life and the lives of many other St. Louis Mercy graduates.

In April of 2008, we had a three-day event in Nashville celebrating our 25th anniversary of the beginning of Mercy Multiplied. I was floored when Kyle and Victoria contacted me to say that they would be coming to our 25th anniversary with their two sons. Even though it had been less than two years since Amber's passing, Kyle and Victoria felt that it was important for them to be there with their family. They even offered to share their painful story about the loss of Amber in an effort to encourage those who need help to get the help they need.

I will never forget that evening on April 18, 2008, as we gathered at the Curb Event Center on the campus of Belmont University. The concert featured major music artists and supporters of Mercy, including CeCe Winans, Natalie Grant, Point of Grace, Barlow Girl, and Israel Houghton. That night of the concert, right before intermission, I took the stage to introduce Kyle and Victoria. They courageously made their way up to the microphone to share their story of losing

Amber, with somewhat heavy hearts, but also seriously wanting to save others from going through the same pain they had been through. All of us in attendance, including the music artists, were amazed at Kyle and Victoria's great strength and compassion as they shared so beautifully from their hearts. It was one of the most moving moments of the whole weekend.

Since that time, Kyle and Victoria have been at every milestone celebration we have had for Mercy. On November 5, 2015, we all gathered in St. Louis at a large hotel ballroom to celebrate the 10-year anniversary of the St. Louis home opening. It was only appropriate that Senator Kyle McCarter and his beautiful wife, Victoria, be the ones to stand before the people that night and share why they support Mercy. They did a beautiful job of encouraging other people to also become financial supporters of Mercy Multiplied. Hearts were so moved as all in attendance knew it had been almost ten years since the loss of their daughter to a drug overdose. People were amazed at the many ways they had been involved in Mercy for an entire decade.

Not only were Kyle and Victoria a regular presence at the home for special events and Mercy graduations, they also served in a variety of ways. Kyle served as a chairman of our community board, and Victoria was regularly involved in special events and volunteer opportunities.

The McCarters have a personal revelation of the scripture in 1 Thessalonians 4:13 which says that as believers, we still have sorrow and we grieve, but not as those who have no hope. They are confident that Amber knew the Lord, and even though she was battling a drug addiction, she had a personal relationship with Christ. That relationship was a big motivating factor in Amber's decision to fill out the Mercy application and get help for her addiction. But unfortunately, she never made it to that point.

It brings great comfort to Kyle and Victoria's hearts, as well as the hearts of their two sons, knowing they will be reunited with Amber in Heaven and they will live together forever with her in eternity. Knowing them so well, they are looking forward to that time, yet their focus is on doing all they can for humanity and for the Kingdom while they are here on this earth.

I am so very thankful for all of my close personal friendships, but these two have a very special place in my heart.

reason

TEN

Franny

Franny was creative from an early age, playing piano by ear at three, and filling notebooks with novels from her own imagination.

"Sing any song and she can play it!" her mother told friends, impressed by her daughter's precociousness.

Franny and her mother often went to the beach, but most of the time her mother worked in their family-owned business. Franny and her brother, who is seven years older, played games together and watched television at home. She felt blessed and comforted to have an older brother who was her best friend.

When she was six, their family moved to a different house and reunited with her father, who struggled with alcohol. Overnight, everything seemed to change. Franny's brother began sexually abusing her when she was only six years of age and telling her it was normal. Her heart hurt and she was very confused over whether he was her protector or predator.

When she was ten, other men began showing up at the house during their parents' work hours. Her brother took money from those men, and Franny became a sexual object for sale.

"Just deal with it," her brother said. "You have no choice."

Franny's brother made a deal with a local gang member, who was now in charge of sex trafficking Franny. He was in his thirties. Sometimes he came over with clients, and sometimes alone. Sometimes he just wanted to sit on the couch and watch TV with Franny. Because she craved a healthy father figure, she tried to convince herself that their activity was not harmful. Her world was divided into two completely separate parts: Life when her parents were home, and everything that happened when they were gone. Whenever her thoughts went back to better days, Franny convinced herself she was wrong—there hadn't been better days. This was life. It was all normal.

Sleep came uneasily. Her mind raced with questions, and she felt fear and pressure to keep the secret from her family.

Serving men like this is my life purpose and my only value, she told herself. *This is what I'm here for.*

Then, after three years, the sex trafficking stopped suddenly. Her brother was arrested for taking part in a gang fight on their block. The older gang leader disappeared from their lives. The end of the sex trafficking seemed like a gift from God, and yet it left a huge gap in Franny's thirteen-year-old life.

Who am I now? she wondered. *My purpose is gone. The only attention and affection I've received from men was in those moments, and from that gang member. What do I do now?*

Grateful that it was over, she also felt emptiness because of the abrupt loss of the relationships that had defined her reality.

Franny had made a habit of skipping school, terrified that a teacher would find out what was going on at home. The school absences led to social workers regularly knocking on their door. At fifteen, Franny dropped out of school entirely.

I don't need a high school diploma, she thought. *My only chance in life is to be a stripper or a prostitute. I don't need a diploma to do that. And I'm not good enough to do anything else.*

Home alone all day, Franny slept as if making up for lost nights. She also drank from the many bottles of alcohol in the house, and self-harmed as her mind tried to make sense of the emotional pain. Sometimes she played the piano like when she was little, but the joy was gone and she no longer felt she deserved something as wonderful as music.

Out of boredom and curiosity, she began walking the streets for hours. Guys pulled up next to her to pick her up, and suddenly she found herself in relationships that only yielded more pain. One guy was violent and tried to slit her throat.

I think my life is a movie, Franny concluded. *There must be cameras around every corner, I just know it. It can't be real. There's just too much pain and destruction going on.*

She also wondered if she was actually in a coma and dreaming everything that happened.

When her mother began attending a new church, Franny reluctantly joined her.

I hate this with all my heart, she thought as the music played and people worshipped. It felt like someone was trying to reach into her heart where she felt unprotected --- *could it be God? That ain't gonna happen,* she thought. *Yes, I believe there's a God, but He only loves and cares about other people—not me. I'm the exception.* Hardening herself against the feelings, she kept her heart cold.

At seventeen, Franny finally told her mom what had happened with her brother, who had been released after more than a year in jail—and their family promptly blew apart. Because her brother had become suicidal and nearly non-functional, their mother asked Franny to live somewhere else while he recovered. Franny moved into the family business's new location, working and sleeping there until she turned eighteen and found an apartment.

Rock bottom was soon to come. Promiscuity, alcohol, drugs, and self-harm produced depression so profound that Franny openly planned her suicide. A relative heard about

Mercy Multiplied on Joyce Meyer's television program and urged Franny to consider it.

I know I need that—or something, Franny thought. *I'm not asking any questions. I'm just going to do it. I have to get out of the place I'm in.*

Franny sent in the application and made a promise to herself: She would try to get help, and if it didn't work, she would take her life.

* * *

Two weeks later, Franny arrived at the St. Louis home—and felt annoyed by everything.

Everyone is so nice, it's disgusting, she thought. *These people are so fake. Seriously? Ugh!*

The passing days didn't improve her outlook.

I hate these rules, she told herself. *I'm a grown woman, so let me do what I'm gonna do! I hate these other girls. I even hate the house dog.*

Franny said little, sat around and stewed.

But the love of God she experienced in worship, and the consistent love from the staff, started to untie the bonds that held her heart. Franny found it difficult to hide after a while.

They know my entire life, all that I have done and all that has been done to me, but they still love me unconditionally, she thought. *I don't get it.*

She realized she was hoping that others would become irritated with her and reject her, fulfilling her expectations. But it never happened.

The St. Louis home sits on top of a huge hill, secluded and surrounded by woods and wildlife.

This is just beautiful, Franny admitted when wandering the grounds. *They keep it immaculate. The food is ridiculous— all organic, expensive, homemade. Who would put together all these resources without even knowing me or these other girls? This is another level of love. But is it real?*

The truth statements the residents are taught to say out loud every day slowly dismantled the stronghold of lies Franny had been living in. She could feel things shifting in her heart as she voiced the words every morning and evening. Lies such as "I am unlovable," "I will never have a family," and "My purpose and value are found in serving men," were replaced with the truths: "I am lovable and loved by God," "I will have a family," "My purpose and value are found in loving God and being in relationship with Him."

It felt like a crawl sometimes, but the melody of her life began to come out again. Soon, Franny began doing something she had rarely done before: writing original songs. Melodies seemed to arrive all in one piece, out of nowhere. Carrying the tune in her head for a week or so, suddenly lyrics would arrive to fit it.

Climb up on My shoulders, let Me show you the world the way it's meant to be seen, she imagined God singing to her. And she replied, *I just want to stay the way that You saw me in Your hands, the way You saw me in the sand, the way that You saw me forever.*

How is this happening? she wondered. *I've never written music before. Now I'm filling notebooks with it!*

Certain songs seemed designed for her to hold onto as she worked through her past. They weren't just random words, but God singing her original identity over her—and affirming how much He loved her. She wrote,

Look up
I'm here
I'll never leave your side
On that you can rely
You may bend, but hold on to Me and you will see
    you won't break
I am here

God showed Franny who she was by showing her who He is. The lie that she didn't deserve to be happy or experience the joy of music faded away. A new intimacy with God was forged deep inside as Franny agreed with the songs of heaven.

One morning, the home director came into Franny's counseling session.

"We got a phone call from a local Dream Center," she said. "They are re-opening their internship program and looking for young women who would be great mentors for troubled teens. I immediately thought of you."

Franny had been pondering a different direction, but after a trial visit, she knew the Dream Center was the place for her. After graduating from Mercy, she moved onto the campus and began working with and mentoring teenage girls. The initial reception from the girls was chilly.

One day, a couple of girls approached Franny. One of them, a fifteen-year-old named Hannah, said, "Me and my friend, Emily, were talking about you. We don't think we're gonna like you very much."

Emily nodded in agreement.

"I just got here," Franny said. "You're not even going to give me a chance?"

They shook their heads.

But when Franny shared parts of her testimony at a youth meeting, the two girls warmed up. Emily began knocking on the door of the women's intern house, where Franny lived.

"Is Franny home?" she asked. "Can she come out and talk?"

In their conversations, Franny discovered that Emily was a sweet, wise and goofy girl who loved to make other people laugh. They noticed similarities in their backgrounds, personalities and outlooks on life. Emily had an older brother with autism and a mother with a drug problem, and was always helping both. She often woke up not knowing where her mother was.

One day, by happenstance, Franny and Emily showed up to a youth gathering with their hair dyed the same color.

"Twins!" they shouted, and the name stuck.

Franny began spending more and more time with Emily and Hannah at the Dream Center, walking around local parks, and going to the popular fish and chicken restaurant nearby.

Both girls went to a performing arts school, and when Franny attended one of Emily's plays, she saw Emily's face light up from the stage when she noticed Franny in the audience. From that point on, Franny committed to attending Emily's performances.

"Okay, twin, I've got another play coming up," Emily would announce, and Franny showed up every time with flowers. Only later did she learn that Emily's mother never came to her shows.

Franny learned that Hannah had experienced similar things as she had in her childhood and was always on guard, even defensive, sometimes pushing Franny away to see if she would reject her. Franny never did.

Hannah had an amazing singing voice, and Franny pushed her to participate in choir, and in the youth praise and worship team at the Dream Center.

"Let your voice be heard. Develop the abilities you have," Franny urged her. "With a voice like that, you can be confident you'll go places."

These girls are really taking my insight and advice seriously, Franny marveled. *That's simply amazing.*

In her second year at the Dream Center, Franny began hearing about a ministry school that is part of Bethel Church in Redding, California, that intrigued her. She watched videos on the Internet and sensed a pull to attend. Then she remembered at Mercy when a visiting minister prayed over each girl. When the minister prayed for Franny, she said: "There's a Bible college, but it's not a traditional Bible college, that God's going to place you in. He's going to place you there to learn more about your calling."

After two years of interning at the Dream Center, Franny was saying good-bye to her family there and moving west to attend the Bethel School of Discipleship. The going-away party was full of tears, but it was just the beginning of a new phase of relationship with Hannah and Emily.

After graduating from high school, Emily enrolled in a state university in Missouri and began pursuing acting. Within a short time she had landed a speaking role in a film. Hannah threw herself into a gospel singing career. Both continue to text Franny several times a week. She will often hear from Emily, "Hey, twin! I miss you so much. Had another audition today!"

In northern California, the music kept flowing as Franny began going through seasons of composing, sometimes composing three songs a day for several months.

This is amazing but tiring! she thought. *But I'm really building a catalog of songs to record.*

Franny graduated from the Bethel School of Discipleship in May of 2018. She has since started her third year with Bethel and is interning for a pastor at Lifehouse Church, a sister church to Bethel. The pastor and her husband have become spiritual parents to Franny, and she couldn't feel more grateful and honored to have them in her life.

In addition to making music, Franny's dream is to start a safe house and shelter for children to come, day or night, to find refuge. Not only that, she wants to offer courses there in fashion, music, theater, writing, and more to draw out and affirm their creativity.

Already, Franny is helping other people rediscover their melodies, the way she rediscovered hers at Mercy Multiplied.

Sex trafficking is an issue that has received a lot of attention over the past few years. As more and more people are learning about this terrible problem, more and more people are wanting to be involved in putting a stop to this horrific evil and being part of the rescue and restoration of its victims.

Human Trafficking is defined by the United Nations Office on Drugs and Crime as "the acquisition of people by improper means such as force, fraud or deception, with the aim of exploiting them" (UNODC, 2018).[1] Sex is just one aspect of human trafficking today. Forced labor and slavery are other forms of trafficking. It's heartbreaking to hear that "human trafficking brings in an estimated $32 billion a year and is tied with arms dealing as the second largest criminal industry in the world (drugs are number 1)" (Archer, 2013).[2]

In the United States, one of the greatest problems with sex trafficking is that most Americans think the issue is only happening in other countries. But "it is estimated that 200,000 women annually are forced into the sex trade in the U.S., and the majority of these are American, not imported from other countries" (2013).2 Many people living in the U.S. are unaware of how this evil is running rampant on their own soil, and when they find out that it is, they often respond with one question: "How?"

We have seen many victims of sex trafficking walk through our doors at Mercy, and Franny's story describes one of many ways that we have seen it happen. Family members exploit and traffick one of their own. It is a heartbreaking reality that someone would be willing to exploit their own family member for a profit, and the hurt and betrayal that the victim experiences as a result is excruciating.

Franny had to process through this hurt and betrayal in her life. As a child, she loved playing games and watching TV with her brother. She considered her brother her "best friend."

---

1 United Nations Office on Drugs and Crime. UNODC on Human Trafficking and Migrant Smuggling. 2018. http://www.unodc.org/unodc /en/human-trafficking/index.html?ref=menuside

2 Archer, Dale. "Human Trafficking in America." *Psychology Today.* Accessed September 5, 2018. https://www.psychologytoday.com/us/blog /reading-between-the-headlines/201304/human-trafficking-in-america

But then the sexual abuse began and eventually her brother handed Franny over to a local gang member to be trafficked. Franny was faced with a deep grief over the loss of a normal, healthy relationship with her big brother.

Through the years of horrific trauma and abuse, the enemy convinced Franny that her life's purpose was to serve men sexually. She was convinced that her identity was in being a sexual object created to be used and abused. Franny learned during her time at Mercy that she had lived under this deception for her entire life. She learned for the first time what her Creator says about her. It was important, though, for Franny to not simply *learn* the truth, but also to practically and daily renew her mind to that truth. She read her truth statements every single day, and over the course of time, she felt the Holy Spirit shifting things in her heart.

Franny also had to walk the difficult, but freeing, road of forgiving herself, as well as others. She learned that forgiving those who had abused her did not mean that she was excusing their behavior or their horrific offenses against her. We sometimes resist forgiveness because it can feel like we are saying that what happened to us was okay. But forgiveness does not place a stamp of approval on the offense. Instead, forgiveness is when we say, "What you did was not okay, but the judgment of your behavior belongs to God, not to me." It's how we hand over the desire for revenge to God, and we trust Him with it. In the end, forgiveness is not about those who have hurt you; it's about *you*—your healing and your freedom.

I am also struck when I read Franny's story how God so powerfully used the unconditional love and grace from the Mercy staff to impact her life. You will hear in the vast majority of testimonies at our Mercy graduations that one of the most impactful pieces of the graduates' journeys was the genuine love that they experienced from the staff. Franny was originally annoyed with how "nice" everyone was; she thought it was all so fake. But as the staff continued to love her and offer God's mercy and grace to her, she shared that the bonds that held her heart started to untie.

We can often get so caught up with saying all of the "right things" to people we know who are struggling. It can be easy to forget that how we treat others is just as, if not more, important than the information we give to them. Colossians 3:14 tells us that above *all*, we are to clothe ourselves with love. We need to love hurting people the same way that Jesus did. He loved them as they were but refused to leave them as they were. We must never underestimate the power of loving others well, of extending grace instead of judgment. God can use these things in a powerful way to shift the hearts of others. As 1 Corinthians 13:8 says, "love never fails."

Franny joined me back in December of 2016 on an international broadcast. She shared her powerful testimony of transformation to a packed studio audience that day, and later with the thousands of people who would watch the show.

I will never forget, as Franny and I were interviewed that night in the studio, how in awe I was. I listened to her share how Jesus Christ had radically healed and transformed her life. I listened to her share the powerful truth about who she is and about who God is. Considering the depth of abuse and pain that she experienced in her past in relation to who she is today, she is the perfect example of what it means to be a new creation in Christ, where the old things have passed away and all things have become new (2 Corinthians 5:17). As I listened to Franny speak that night, it was as if none of this had ever even happened. There wasn't an ounce of residue left from her past. It profoundly impacted me; the unbelievable transformation in her life could not be denied!

It's incredible to know the depth of hurt and trauma and abuse that Franny suffered, and to see how fully restored and redeemed her life is today. And it is such a joy to see how Mercy is truly being multiplied through Franny now as she ministers to girls like Hannah and Emily. Her heart to help others and her desire to start a safe house back in her home city is amazing and such a testament to the healing and freedom that God has brought to her life. This kind of life transformation cannot be explained outside of the miraculous power of Christ!

reason

ELEVEN

Emily

Emily grew up in a Christian home in Oklahoma City with amazing parents and an older brother, Drew, who was her best friend. Her father told her many times, "I know all kids are special, but when you were born I said out loud, 'This girl is so special, she's going to do something big.'" As a young child, Emily's mom would sit and talk with her and read to her from an illustrated Bible. In her teen years, Emily enjoyed church youth group, especially worship time.

But school was another story. Kids made fun of her and excluded her from their cliques. To make it worse, in high school, her brother, Drew became one of the popular kids just as Emily began struggling with a mysterious health issue that caused lethargy and weight gain. By her freshman year of high school, Emily was sleeping 16 hours a day because of the health issue and was known at school as "Drew's sister." Desperate for friends, Emily tried everything: kindness, forgiveness, trusting everyone and being perfect at everything. None of it worked.

Everyone thinks I'm happy because I smile and laugh a lot, but I feel so stupid and unloved, Emily thought many times. She made a point to hide her pain even from her parents.

An ultrasound on her neck finally revealed hypothyroidism, a condition in which the thyroid gland doesn't produce enough thyroid hormone, causing fatigue and weight gain. Medication slowly alleviated the problem, but Emily was a sophomore and the pain of social rejection had already gone deep. Unlike Drew, she refused to go out partying and drinking, leaving her mostly alone.

My entire life takes place in Drew's shadow, she thought. *I don't even have a name to these people—I'm just "Drew's sister."*

I wish I could run away and be my own person and figure out who I am.

An inner voice seemed to agree, whispering, *You're stupid. You're not worth anything. You'll never have friends.* Emily agreed with those thoughts and they became her reality. Outwardly, she maintained a happy façade, but her mother could tell that something was wrong. When her mother asked, Emily assured her everything was fine.

One summer in high school, Emily met some new guys at a nearby lake and found the perfect opportunity to craft a new persona.

I don't have to be "Drew's sister" here, she thought. *I can be who I want to be. I can even start drinking, like they do.*

The lake became her weekend hangout, and she started drinking to the point of blacking out. The people she partied with were just as broken as she was, and craving relationships, Emily took on the role of caretaker of damaged people.

They need me, she thought. *I can help them. I know their pain.*

Back home, a girl named Molly started showing up at the house. She was Drew's girlfriend, older than Emily by a couple of years, and the definition of "cool" in Emily's eyes. But Molly and Drew were using hard drugs. Desperate to gain Molly's approval, Emily latched onto her. She also adopted Molly's lifestyle. Emily had taken a prescription drug one time that seemed to snap her out of lethargy and give her incredible energy.

"I would love some more of that drug," Emily mentioned to Molly innocently one day.

"I can find you something better than that," Molly promised. That night at a local pool hall, one of Molly's friends introduced Emily to crystal meth in the bathroom while a guy Emily had just met banged on the door shouting, "Don't do it, Emily! You'll ruin your life." In a way, his words were prophetic.

Emily felt confident and excited about life while high, and found herself awake for three days straight. Someone mentioned that meth caused rapid weight loss, and as she used more, Emily saw it was true. She was becoming thin and socially accepted, which was what she had wanted.

Emily was living in increasing bondage to the drug and its effects. She soon dropped out of school, moved out of her parents' house and began living out of her truck, holding jobs as she was able. Her revolving friend group consisted of random people at the pool hall, local gang members, fellow drug users and those who had houses or apartments where they could use. Unlike many of them, Emily was not into living a reckless lifestyle, or stealing, or letting her appearance go. Rather, she dressed well, put on make-up and seemed "normal" from the outside looking in. More than once, fellow users asked if she was an undercover cop.

This isn't who I am, she reminded herself many times. *I'm not the girl who lives on the streets and uses meth with strangers. I'm the girl who grew up in a Christian home and who cries when worship music plays.*

But the energy, social acceptance, thinness and confidence kept her in bondage to the crystal meth.

Danger soon reared its head. One night at the pool hall, Emily felt warned by the internal voice of God that something bad was about to happen. Moments later, while she was sitting in a parked car with a friend, a stranger opened the door and shot her friend in the hand. The bullet went clean through. Emily fled before anything could happen to her.

That could have been me, she thought, heart racing. It wasn't the last time she was close to danger.

Emily suspected that many of the people she hung out with were deep into gang life and crime. When in strange hotel rooms and apartments, she kept herself from drifting off with the thought, *If I fall asleep here, they may kill me. I don't trust anyone I'm with.*

Pride kept her from returning home, as did her commitment to feeling beautiful, confident and loved—things she thought only drugs could give her.

I'm never going back to what I was before, she promised herself, *but I'm so naïve and trusting, it's going to hurt me someday. I've already had so much stolen from me and been in danger for my life. Some people know how to live the street life, but I don't think I do. It terrifies me.*

Finally, when Emily was 18, her parents successfully intervened and sent her to Florida for a week at a rehab facility. The cost was significant, but the results were lacking. So they sent her to a rehab center in Taos, New Mexico, a small, mountainous enclave of earthy people and Bohemian lifestyles. After finishing the program, Emily stayed in town and roomed with a friend with the shared commitment of staying clean.

Sex became Emily's new "drug", and a promiscuous lifestyle seemed to supply the acceptance and love she desired. Then she learned that their downstairs neighbor was a cocaine dealer. Emily and her roommate succumbed, and as they used, Emily's feelings of invincibility returned. She bounced from one job to another, repeatedly fired, but more committed to being high than being employed.

She met a recovering heroin addict, Luke, at a substance abuse recovery meeting, and found in him a kindred soul drawn to damaged people.

"We can fix each other," he said. "We'll do this together. We'll stay clean. I'll help you, and you'll help me."

But Emily was committed to staying high, and her addiction became his. Soon they were living together as he spent thousands on cocaine for both of them and eventually lost his job.

Their relationship was based on a destructive pattern of emotional extremes. Physical altercations, yelling, and cops responding to domestic violence calls became common. So did "making up" where romantic feelings seemed to go as deep as the passionate anger just moments before.

This must be what love feels like, Emily thought as the cycle continued.

In her room sat a Bible and a daily devotional book which Emily repeatedly promised to read, but never did. The Bible was a constant reminder of the life she knew she should be living.

I know it's the right way to live, she told herself. *But I'm enjoying my friends and the feelings the drugs give me. I don't really need to change.*

The violence only escalated. One night, Emily cut a hole in a bedroom door with a set of pliers after Luke locked himself in to do heroin.

Another weekend, she slept with a guy she met at a party, and when Luke found out, he burned her clothes in the back yard. Emily came home to find her newly-purchased clothes and other clothing blackened and useless. The police arrived. In retaliation, Emily broke Luke's expensive sunglasses, a gift from his brother. Then they apologized and made up as if nothing had happened.

Over 500 miles away, Emily's mom suspected that Emily was not doing well. She could only rely on what Emily told her, but she sensed that Emily was not being truthful about her lifestyle. In early 2008, she called Emily to tell her about Mercy Multiplied.

"You need to look up this website and click on the testimonies," her mother said.

When Emily did, she began sobbing.

I feel their pain, their lostness, the dark spot they're in, she thought. *Even now I just want to fade away and disappear sometimes. I don't think I can stay safe much longer the way I'm living.*

"I need to go there," she told her mom, and she began the application process.

A toxic mix of prescription medicines and alcohol drove Emily to a violent extreme one night. Fighting as usual with Luke, he began ignoring her. Emily went into the kitchen, grabbed a knife and slit her wrists to try to get his attention. Paper towels helped stop the bleeding, but when she woke up the next morning, she could see her ligaments within the wounds.

This is bad, she thought on her way to the hospital. *Even though I was high, I could have killed myself. I'm putting myself in so many bad situations. If I don't go somewhere I will end up dead.*

Within two weeks, in July of 2008, Emily's parents moved her out of Taos and in with her aunt and uncle in Kansas while she waited for a spot at Mercy Multiplied to open up. When it did, Emily was less than enthusiastic.

I don't want to feel controlled, she fumed.

But when she stepped into the doors of Mercy in January of 2009, a feeling of complete peace came over her. She was shocked when all of the residents came down to the front lobby to greet her.

Whoa! This is amazing, she thought. *This is it. This is the life I'm supposed to live.*

Over the next six months, God turned Emily's life completely around. She miraculously experienced no cravings or withdrawals from leaving drugs behind. Rather, she reconnected with worship music, and would lay on the floor singing and weeping to worship songs.

Oh my gosh, God does love me, she thought. *He loves me so much and there's nothing that will change that. Nothing will take away God's love for me.*

She filled notebooks with notes on every lesson, every sermon at church, every testimony, every DVD, every meaningful class or conversation, diligently writing the key points of what she learned.

A prophetic minister visiting the home one time prayed over each girl and told Emily, "I see a bouncing ball going every which way. That's you. You were going all over the place. You're a light and you smile all the time, but underneath that smile you were hurting. While you were hurting God was still there with you."

That's exactly who I was, Emily thought.

"There's one incident that you keep replaying in your head over and over again," the minister continued.

Emily knew exactly which incident she was referring to.

"God is saying it's under the blood of Christ and you don't have to think about it again," the minister said.

Everything she says is right! Emily marveled. *This is amazing.*

Phone calls with her mother were completely different than before.

"Mom, I just listened to this audio book and it's incredible," Emily said, almost breathlessly. "God is so good!"

"Emily," her mom finally said, "You are day and night different from before."

Every morning, Emily walked around the parking lot speaking her truth statements and reading *God's Creative Power* by Charles Capps. She learned about breaking soul ties and generational patterns. She repented of befriending people out of need for social acceptance, and allowing their bad habits to become her own.

Most of all, she recommitted her life to Christ and His calling on her life. Her only stipulation was that she wasn't moving back to Oklahoma.

I'm scared of using again, she told God. *I'll go anywhere but back home.*

One day while she was listening to praise and worship music, God spoke to her heart, "You are moving back to Oklahoma. I have delivered you from drugs." Emily never felt the slightest draw to drugs, alcohol or cigarettes after that.

Upon graduating from Mercy Multiplied in July of 2009, she moved in with her parents and attended a Christian art school. A friend there strategically invited Emily to a game night at her house to meet a certain young man, Chad, a strongly committed Christian.

"I don't want to be in a relationship," Emily told the friend preemptively. "I want to figure out where to go with my life."

But that night, Chad saw Emily and immediately knew

they would be married. They began seeing each other, and five months after they met, on Mother's Day of 2010, he proposed. They were married the following January.

Marriage should have been the fulfillment of many dreams, but instead, Emily began sabotaging their relationship. She only knew what false "love" felt like in a violent, rebellious manner. She tried to provoke fights with Chad, who was by nature more even-keeled and peaceable. With nothing to "fix" in their relationship, Emily felt as if love were missing.

"I don't love you like I loved Luke," she told Chad, trying to draw him into a fight while also explaining her own feelings.

"Do you just want to argue?" Chad asked.

Well, yes! Emily thought to herself. *If our relationship breaks, then I can fix it and show you I love you.*

To her, love began after the yelling and screaming and violence, when there was something to apologize for. Chad seldom took the bait, but her words wounded him, and bitterness set in. Soon, their original feelings for each other seemed to have vanished.

I deserve to be left, Emily thought, lying in bed at night. *I've basically tried to drive him away, but he keeps sticking with me.*

The next day she apologized, but "I'm sorry" only went so far. Emily tried to bottle up her feelings again, as when she was younger, but confusion and guilt only stewed inside of her.

On September 15, 2012, Emily gave birth to a daughter, Lily, but the joy of having their first child was diminished by the ever-increasing struggles in their marriage. Chad and Emily eventually separated and began individual counseling to try to salvage their marriage. In her sessions, Emily realized she had already been given the keys to victory at Mercy Multiplied.

I experienced the love of God there, she reminded herself. *I learned at Mercy that no matter what the enemy tries to throw at me, I was equipped with the tools to handle any problems. I took care of a lot of things from my past there, and I can use those same tools to enforce what I know to be true in this situation.*

With great intensity and prayer, Emily confronted the lies in her own soul about the nature of love, and the nature of her relationship with Luke and with Chad. She remembered from her time at Mercy about the importance of recognizing lies and replacing them with truth. So using truth statements about her marriage, she replaced deception with rock-solid reality, building a foundation in Christ for her and Chad to stand on.

Chad, too, received healing from his counseling sessions which led to reconciliation with Emily. After two months of being separated, they moved back in together, into a new house, and began walking in real love with one another. Emily learned that love didn't have to be defined by violent fighting and making up.

The result was a beautiful, growing relationship they hadn't been able to imagine before. They began talking daily about how much they loved each other and connecting on a deeper level. Even their relatives were amazed by the transformation in their marriage. Instead of firing harsh words back and forth, they found joy in treating each other with respect and tenderness.

"It's amazing how much grace and mercy has fallen on our marriage," Emily says. "We've even talked about doing marriage counseling for *others* one day!"

Emily and Chad had their second daughter, Isabelle, in January of 2015 and their third daughter, Arya, almost exactly three years later.

In November of 2017, Emily took another big step and became a merchandiser for a specialty dress-maker, hosting parties and selling vibrantly-colored dresses to young girls. Watching the girls light up in their beautiful clothes means much more to Emily than having a nice outfit. It's a way of clothing girls in their true identity in Christ, which is of infinite worth. Someday, Emily wants to speak encouragement to groups of girls as part of the calling she has felt on her life from the beginning.

Emily is certain of one thing: "Nothing would have transformed my life but the power of Christ and God's Word. The only thing that worked for me was Him."

———

Emily's story is one of many examples of a young woman who grew up in a supportive home with loving parents. She wasn't abused or neglected as a child. Yet she still experienced the pain and difficulty of living in a broken world. She faced the hurt of rejection by kids at school. She believed the lies of the enemy about who she was and was desperate to feel included and have friends.

I have had countless conversations with mothers and fathers racking their brains to figure out "where they went wrong" with their kids. Their child may be struggling with any number of issues, but the parents assume that it's *their* fault. However, Emily's story reminds us that a mother and father can do all that they know to give their child a safe and loving environment, but it doesn't automatically mean that their child will never struggle.

Of course there are no two people on the planet who are perfect parents. We all have areas where we struggle, and these areas of struggle will undoubtedly affect our parenting. So it's important to never stop growing as individuals and allowing God to bring us to new levels of healing and freedom in our own lives. Because as we become healthier people, we will be healthier parents. However, just as there are no perfect parents, there are also no perfect kids. And while God calls all parents to do their best to love and encourage and raise their children in a healthy, safe environment, we must also realize that we cannot control our children. We must love them, and we must be willing to surrender them into His hands.

If you are a parent and you have a child that is struggling, the enemy will try to heap shame and condemnation on you as their mother or father. If you see legitimate areas where you need to offer an apology to your child (whether young or old), I encourage you to humbly offer the apology. It is one of the most powerful things that you can give to your child. Repent to God and to your child as needed. Seek to continually grow and become a healthier parent. But then extend to yourself the same grace that God extends to you. Shame is a powerful tool of the enemy, and it will not help you or your children.

When the enemy attacks you with shame, run to the place where your shame is covered: Jesus Christ. Isaiah 53 says that He bore our shame on the cross, so we now have a legal right to use our authority as believers to command shame to go, in

Jesus' Name. Because of what Jesus did on the cross, shame no longer has power over us.

Emily had wonderful, loving parents, but the enemy used other painful circumstances in her life to convince her of lies about who she was. The enemy attacked her self-worth and she tried every possible means of being accepted by her peers. Her desperation for relationships led her to take on the role of "caretaker." She was drawn toward hurting and struggling people, believing that her purpose was to help them.

Emily would eventually have to learn a hard lesson: she couldn't "fix" anyone. So many people have big hearts to help people who are struggling, which is a wonderful thing. God has called us to be a light in this dark world. However, He has *not* called us to be anyone's savior. We are not called to be Jesus; that seat is already taken!

If you are in a relationship with someone who is struggling, I encourage you to always remember that the weight of change is on the person you are helping, not on you. Don't let others hand you their responsibilities. They must be the ones to choose healing and freedom in their own lives. If you think you can fix another person, you will experience a lot of heartache and frustration.

The hurt and deception that had so defined Emily's life eventually spiraled to the point that she was addicted to drugs and living a promiscuous lifestyle. Her dating relationship with Luke was extremely unhealthy, and this led to a whole new set of struggles in Emily's life. We read in her story that their relationship was "based on a destructive pattern of emotional extremes."

One of the keys to freedom that the young women at Mercy learn about is how to find freedom from oppression. We define oppression as "pressure" and anything that the enemy is able to bring into our lives through our choices or the choices of others in the form of habits, addictions, thought patterns, and even unhealthy relationships. Emily's relationship with Luke was the epitome of an unhealthy relationship that opened the door for oppression in Emily's life.

While God created us to have relationships and connect with one another in healthy ways, some relationships become attached in ways outside of His design, forming an unhealthy or ungodly emotional attachment. We share about these types of unhealthy attachments in Mercy's *Keys to Freedom* study:

> *Relationships that position us to become more of who God created us to be and allow us to reciprocate this for others are the relationships we want to cultivate in our lives. The easiest way to identify the health of our attachment is by examining the fruit of it. When healthy, the fruit of our lives intersecting with others will always reflect God's heart and purpose for connection. However, sometimes we have the wrong influences in our lives, and we can become connected in unhealthy ways through various means. Influences such as manipulation, intimidation, unhealthy emotional dependency, control and violation can all result in unhealthy attachments.*

It's pretty clear when we look at Emily's story that her relationship with Luke contained all of the things listed above. Another way that unhealthy ties can be formed is through sexual interactions outside the boundaries of marriage. God's design for sex is that it would bond two people together in a lifetime commitment to one another. It's to be a seal of a covenant marriage. Unfortunately, when people move outside of those boundaries, that bond can create an unhealthy "soul tie." For many young women who have lived promiscuous lifestyles before coming to Mercy, it's as if part of their soul is still connected to everyone they've been with sexually. There is then a need to address and break those ties so that they can be fully restored, as soul ties can have a lifelong negative impact on your life and your relationships.

One of the most important keys to Emily's freedom was to identify and address the unhealthy emotional attachment she'd had with Luke. If you recognize unhealthy emotional attachments in your own life, I encourage you to address them through prayer, and through counseling if needed, and then set boundaries as the Holy Spirit leads. In some relationships, like Emily and Luke's, it may mean a clean break entirely, especially if it has been sinful and destructive. In others, it may mean redefining the relationship by setting new boundaries. As we mention in *Keys to Freedom*, "You have the authority and ability to choose who and what you are connected to."

Lastly, I love how Emily's story reminds us that freedom is not a one-time event; it's a process. Emily did not leave the Mercy program as a perfect person, but she did leave equipped. Our God is a God of process, and after Emily graduated from Mercy and got married, the Lord brought up new areas where He needed to work in her life. I am so proud of how Emily persevered through her difficulties after Mercy. She remembered the tools she had learned and she put them to work. She sought additional counseling. She allowed the Holy Spirit to continue the good work that He had started in her life.

He promises to do the same for you! Philippians 1:6 tells us that the One who started a good work in each of us will carry it on to completion. So don't grow weary or discouraged in your own journey to freedom. The God who radically transformed Emily's life is no respecter of persons. What He does for one, He wants to do for all, but you must be willing to make choices to see the changes that you desire. You must make the choice to commit your life and surrender your heart to Him, and you can know the same life and freedom that Emily found!

reason

TWELVE

Matilda

When Matilda was young, she, her sister and her neighborhood friends played fairies, warriors and princesses in the woods near their house in suburban St. Louis. They built forts from sticks and branches, and pretended they were mermaids in the community pool. Matilda enjoyed being outside so much that she only came in when her parents called for her.

At home, the atmosphere was not so joyful. Her mom worked a lot. Her father drank heavily and came and went unpredictably. Sometimes he was gone for long stretches of time and nobody knew why. On weekends when he was home, his brother came over and they drank together. When Matilda was five, her uncle began sexually abusing her when her dad was too inebriated to notice. An older, female friend and Matilda's brother's friend also began abusing her. Sexual activity became a weekly part of her life for the next six years.

The abuse stopped gradually, but the confusion had just begun. Matilda's mind was overcome with shame, self-hatred and twisted thoughts she didn't know how to handle. She started drinking alcohol at 13, and to gain some sense of control, she restricted her food intake and took laxatives to make herself thinner.

Night terrors began, and in an attempt to exorcise the pain and fear, Matilda began scratching herself with fingernail clippers, scissors, bobby pins, nails—whatever was available. With a hammer she hit her legs until they bruised. While smoking—a habit she took up in her early teens—she held a lighter to her arms and legs.

This is demonic, she thought, feeling pain but not stopping. *At least the emotional pain inside of me is being momentarily drowned out by the intensity of the physical pain from intentionally hurting myself. I deserve this. This is what I get for what happened to me.*

Matilda was so starved for positive attention that she became bitter and mean, making fun of kids at school just for approval. Bracelets covered her arms—and her wounds. "You're a freak," schoolmates told her when they caught sight of the scars. So Matilda wore bandages instead and made excuses: "They're from my dog." "I got the scratches while cooking." "I fell asleep and fell on a pin cushion."

She controlled her food—and food controlled her. Keeping track of the thinnest people in her school, sometimes she asked with apparent innocence, "How much does everybody weigh?"

I'm going to be the thinnest and smallest of anyone, she promised herself.

Friends noticed, and laughed at her: "You're so skinny. You're anorexic."

"No, I'm not," Matilda replied, but she knew where the most obscure bathroom on campus was and used it to purge. Pills, taken from her parents' supply of prescription medicines, had ruined her stomach lining, and she developed five large ulcers. She could barely digest food. When a teacher caught her throwing up in the bathroom, it meant counseling. Grudgingly, Matilda admitted her eating disorder, but not the sexual abuse.

That was my fault. I brought it on somehow, she convinced herself of the horror she had experienced.

In high school, she discovered that her father had had another family in secret that he had recently abandoned. Matilda met her half-sister on Facebook.

This is the ultimate betrayal, Matilda thought. *He's been lying to us all this time. I can never forgive him for this.*

As her parents headed for divorce, Matilda spent most of her time at friends' houses and at parties. One night, Matilda volunteered to be a designated driver because her best friend had a nice convertible. Two guys they had never met approached them at the party and offered them smoothies.

"There's no alcohol in this, right?" Matilda asked.

"No, you're fine," they assured her.

The guys kept refilling their drinks. Soon, Matilda was seeing strange things.

What is going on? Matilda thought in a deepening haze.

She woke up in a bed upstairs. Beside her was her friend. Groggily, they opened their eyes.

"What happened?" the friend asked.

"We have to get out of here," Matilda said. Realizing they had been raped, they quickly grabbed their clothes, ran to the car and drove to her friend's house.

"What do we do?" they asked each other. "Who were those guys?"

"I don't know, but we have to tell our boyfriends," the friend said.

She and Matilda called their boyfriends that day to relay what had happened—and both boys broke up with them. From that day forward, the girls felt they had no choice but to act like it had never happened.

I hate myself and my life, Matilda thought. *I want to die.*

The rape brought back tormenting thoughts from her childhood abuse, even though her uncle's abuse had been discovered and he was serving five years in prison. Certain places, songs, smells and articles of clothing triggered terrifying flashbacks. Panic attacks led to seizures.

God put me on this earth to be a sex toy for other people,

Matilda concluded. *If that's the point of my life, I'm done. I can't live like this.*

One night she parked her old, beat-up Jeep on the train tracks and waited for a train to come. When the train's headlight appeared, speeding toward her in the dark, she thought, *No, this isn't how I want to do this—too gruesome,* and pulled off the tracks.

A large number of pills from various doctors, counselors and her parents' house were readily available—pills for panic attacks, anxiety, insomnia, depression and pain. In an attempt to end her life, she took several handfuls one night, but only got a visit to the hospital.

Turning to marijuana, more prescription pills and even cocaine, Matilda started dealing drugs with her newly-discovered half-sister as a "business partner." They grew marijuana in her half-sister's apartment, sold it, then stole it back from the people they sold it to, and sold it again. By now, Matilda was living out of her car while still in high school.

You know what? she thought one afternoon when the flashbacks of her past abuse were especially bad. *Pills didn't work. I'm going to jump off a bridge.*

She found an overpass over a busy highway and sat on the edge, legs dangling in the air. The sun faded into the horizon. Cars, trucks and big rigs swooshed below at highway speeds.

If I sneeze, I'm going over, she thought.

Across the overpass, people jogged by with little more than a glance, even though Matilda was openly cutting herself in a final defiance of the world. Then a familiar voice came.

"Hey, what are you doing? What's going on? Matilda?"

It was her high school music teacher. Rapidly, the woman pulled Matilda off the ledge, as Matilda struggled.

"You're not stopping me," Matilda said. "I have to get it over with."

"No!" said the woman, and grabbed her arm and wouldn't let go. "You're coming with me."

Matilda wasn't strong enough to resist, though she tried. Back at the teacher's car, the police soon arrived.

"She's coming to my house," the teacher said. "I'll take care of her tonight."

While waiting, Matilda had opened up about the haunting flashbacks. The teacher took Matilda's cigarettes, pocket knife and anything else vaguely harmful. At her house they watched a Disney movie until Matilda fell asleep on the couch.

The incident led to several weeks of outpatient rehabilitation, which didn't do anything to help. After a particularly discouraging counseling session, in which Matilda felt the counselor had violated trust by telling others about her problems, she stormed out to her Jeep. In the center console she kept multiple pill bottles, just in case one day proved too rough.

This is it, she told herself. *It ends here. God won't be able to torture me anymore.*

She poured the pills into her hands and prepared to swallow them. Suddenly, a presence filled the car. Matilda looked around her, in the back seat, and under the seats. She saw nothing, but the peace was so strong it seemed tangible.

I'm freaking out, Matilda thought. *I know there's someone in here.*

Then a voice came, not audibly, though it may as well have been: *Just give Me one month,* it said.

The voice filled her with such hope. Somehow, she knew it was Jesus.

"Okay," she responded to Him. "I'll give You a month. But

that's all. If You don't do anything for me, I'm done with life."

She put the pills back in the center console and drove home.

Her mother had met a woman named Donna, the senior pastor of a local church, and when Donna met Matilda for coffee she said firmly, "You need to go to Mercy. It will be really good for you."

I don't want to go, Matilda thought, *but it is free of charge. We've been paying so much for counseling and out-patient treatment. Might as well try it.*

Remembering her bargain with Jesus, Matilda made up her mind to apply to Mercy Multiplied. Two weeks later, her mom was driving her to the home in Monroe, Louisiana.

Let's see if this works, Matilda thought. She had a backup plan if it didn't: move to California with her half-sister to deal drugs. They had worked it all out, how to use Matilda's medical diagnoses to secure pills and medical marijuana they could re-sell. Her half-sister had even bought a plane ticket.

The first night at Mercy didn't feel promising. Surrounded by new people, and struggling with anxiety and flashbacks, Matilda cried herself to sleep.

Why am I here? she wondered. *Why am I even doing this?*

But the next few days felt so saturated in unconditional love, from the staff and others, that Matilda asked, "What do you people want from me? Why are you so nice?" Inside she was thinking, *This is awesome. They keep loving me no matter what I act like.* For the first time she was receiving love without having to earn it.

On her first Sunday there, the residents went to a smaller, older church, not unlike the one Matilda had attended occasionally with her mother.

"If anyone wants prayer, come up and I'll pray for you," the pastor said toward the end of the service.

Without thinking it through, Matilda went forward and stood in front. The pastor smiled and began to pray for her. Overwhelming peace blanketed her—then she heard an audible voice say loudly and triumphantly, "It is finished!" The powerful voice rang through her entire being, from her physical body to the depths of her spirit. Her eyes popped open and she looked around.

"Did you hear that?" she asked a girl next to her.

"Hear what?" the girl asked.

"Didn't anyone hear that?" Matilda asked. "Who said that?"

They couldn't have missed it, she thought. *It sounded like a trumpet blast.*

By now she was weeping, because the voice had changed something inside her, and she knew it.

Whatever this is, I want it, she thought.

From that day on, Matilda never experienced another anxiety attack. She promptly forgot about her backup plan.

Friendships bloomed and Bible teaching and worship shifted her thinking about God. Simply having fun with other girls brought back an innocence she had longed for. For the first time, Matilda felt understood, not like "the crazy one" in her world.

Joyce Meyer's testimony captivated her.

Here's someone who went through the same things I did, Matilda thought. *Now she's doing awesome and living in freedom. Tell me more!*

Matilda loved listening to Joyce Meyer teachings, drinking in the healing words and Joyce's example of transformation. Writing and declaring truth statements was hugely impactful, as was listening to the testimonies of young women who were graduating. She also learned that what she had been told before—"Once an addict, always an addict"—was nothing more than a lie.

A few months into her stay, Matilda started thinking about rebuilding a relationship with her dad. It would have seemed impossible just months ago, but her heart was tender and she wanted to share the mercy she was receiving. Matilda went to her room and prayed, "God, I want to walk out forgiveness toward my dad, even though he hurt us and lied and didn't protect us. Help me to do that."

Matilda's first conversation with her dad lasted all of a hundred seconds, but at least it happened. She thanked God and prayed, "I believe we will have more than a two-minute conversation. I declare we will have a five-minute conversation!"

The next time they talked, Matilda's openness to relationship surprised him.

"Call me next Saturday," she told him at the end.

"Really?" he said. "Okay, I'll call you."

"I love you," she said.

"Oh . . . okay," he said, and they hung up, but Matilda was smiling. They had talked for nearly ten minutes.

A few weeks later, she ended with the same thing: "I love you."

"I love you, too," he replied.

Tears moistened her eyes as she hung up the phone. It wasn't that he had changed overnight, but that God was somehow working through her situation to restore all aspects of her life—including the lives of those she loved.

Matilda was fascinated to learn that Jesus—the Man she had first encountered in her Jeep—was all about love, redemption and healing, nothing like the perfectionist, angry deity she grew up imagining. Being honest and real with Him was not only allowed but encouraged.

"You don't have to hide anymore," her counselor told her. "If you're angry and need to lay that out, do it. He knows what you're thinking. Let Him meet you where you're at."

"God, why did this happen?" Matilda asked time and again when praying through hurts, and each time He brought peace and seemed to whisper, "I've got you. I love you." Though some questions went unanswered, peace was an answer enough: It would be okay. She could be healed without understanding everything.

I've always been afraid of being vulnerable, she thought. *But Jesus was the most vulnerable when He hung on the cross, and His vulnerability brought healing. I think that's what's happening to me.*

She had met with many counselors before coming to Mercy, and nothing changed. The difference now, she concluded, was that it wasn't just her and a counselor—Jesus was in the room as well.

When Matilda and three other girls learned they would graduate in a few weeks, they ran around the halls jumping up and down and hollering with excitement, like little kids playing in the safety of a Father's love.

* * *

After graduating from Mercy in April of 2013, Matilda moved back to St. Louis to live with a woman in Donna's church and walk out her freedom. Within a little while she was inundated with new, godly friends. The church, and those friendships, were critical to strengthening her foundation in Christ, and many people poured into her life through active mentoring, occasional coffees, Bible studies and just hanging out.

A guy in the young adults group caught her attention. *He is a really good guy and loves Jesus,* Matilda thought. After a year of friendship, they began dating. For the first time, Matilda felt safe with a man.

They dated for two years and then one day, Matilda's boyfriend sent her on a scavenger hunt around St. Louis to some of her favorite places and memorable locations from their dating relationship. At each location, a good friend of Matilda's was holding a handwritten note from Matilda's boyfriend filled with encouragement, love and fun memories they had made together. The scavenger hunt included a trip to a nail salon and spa room, and ended in a beautiful park where her boyfriend proposed to her. A catered dinner with close family and friends rounded out the amazing day, which remains forever etched in Matilda's memory.

A few short months after the proposal, they were married, and Matilda carefully took notice of the strong, godly marriages around her at church.

Ah, so that's what a healthy marriage looks like, she observed. *That's what a wife does, and that's what a husband does. Good to know!*

About a year into their marriage, she and her husband felt called to join a team that was planting a church in downtown St. Louis. 80 people showed up to the first public service, surprising them all. One visitor came forward with a tumor, and Matilda and other team members prayed for healing. The woman woke up the next morning to find that the tumor was gone. A man requested prayer for sleep problems and racing thoughts. After that day, his mind settled down completely and he slept through the night.

Matilda and her husband are still serving as leaders at that church. God has opened numerous doors for Matilda to share her testimony both there and in other settings.

"Society's views on sex are twisted, and so many people have been sexually abused," Matilda said recently. "God intended sex to be something beautiful and special between a husband and a wife. I don't leave the sexual abuse aspect out of my story because I want people to experience the same healing and freedom that I walk in today."

As they pray for God to move mightily in the city of St. Louis and for people to encounter His love, their church is growing quickly and already needs a new facility. Matilda has shared her story with more than a thousand people, and each time it has prompted someone to go to Mercy. She continues to help walk young women through eating disorders, anger, pain from sexual abuse, anxiety and more.

In February of 2018, Matilda was hired to work part-time as the Program Assistant at the St. Louis Mercy home. She assists with various needs in the home, including answering the phone, receiving visitors and guests, and anything else that is needed.

"I absolutely love my job," Matilda told us recently. "I never knew I could love a job so much. Getting to love on the young women at Mercy and be a part of the vision is amazing. I look forward to going to work. The staff are beautiful lovers of Jesus and I am truly honored to be part of the team.

Matilda added, "It is always God's will to bring freedom. I never thought I would be getting to work at Mercy, but God's plans for our lives are always so much better than what we can think or dream. The testimony of what Jesus does is powerful!"

——————————

The amount of abuse that Matilda suffered as a child is almost unimagineable. Sexual abuse from family members and friends was a normal part of her childhood, and she was eventually raped in her high school years.

Child sexual abuse is a major issue in the world today. In the U.S. alone, 1 in 3 girls and 1 in 6 boys is a victim of child sexual abuse (DHHS, 2018).3 And the effects of childhood abuse are significant—from drug use to self-harm to eating disorders to suicidal or depressive thoughts. If you take a look at Matilda's story, you see that she literally struggled with everything on this list.

Sexual abuse is a horrifying reality, and thousands upon thousands of people today are living in the shame and torment of their unspoken secret. Any time you are manipulated or coerced into engaging in any type of sexual activity, that is abuse. And it doesn't have to include intercourse to qualify as "abuse."

If you have experienced sexual abuse, no matter how recently or how long ago, the first step to finding healing

——————————

3   U.S. Department of Health & Human Services, Administration for Children and Families, Administration on Children, Youth and Families, Children's Bureau. (2018). Child maltreatment 2016. Available from https://www.acf.hhs.gov/cb/research-data-technology/statistics-research /child-maltreatment.

is acknowledging the abuse for exactly what it was. It may seem easier to push those horrible memories to the back of your mind or even convince yourself that what occurred was normal or was your own fault. But keeping your secret in the dark will keep you in bondage to your past. Denying the reality of the abuse will deny God access to your heart to bring healing and freedom.

I also encourage you to share your experience with a trusted family member, friend, pastor or counselor. Tell someone who you know can help you process the pain and expose the lies that the enemy may have bombarded you with. If you are presently experiencing abuse, you must tell someone you trust in order to get out of this unhealthy situation. God never intended for you to be taken advantage of, and by exposing the truth of what is happening, you can prevent the person who is hurting you from hurting others as well!

Matilda experienced something that is very common for victims of sexual abuse: anger at God. She learned, though, that she had to bring her anger and hurt and questions directly to Him. She learned that He would not only allow her to question Him, He actually *wanted* it. He wanted her to come to Him in her raw, angry, vulnerable state, because He desired to minister to her heart in that place. And He wants the same with all of us.

As Matilda openly and honestly poured out her doubts, questions and anger to God, she learned about His true nature. She learned that He was not the author of her abuse, and it was not His will for her to be used and abused. She learned that, as James 1:17 tells us, every good and perfect gift comes from God, so this was obviously not from Him. Matilda realized that she was hurt by people who were wrongly using their free will. But thankfully, she had a good Father who loved her enough to help her put the shattered pieces of her heart and life back together.

Matilda didn't specifically receive answers to all of her questions, but she did receive Him. At the end of the day, God knows that the remedy for our broken hearts is not for all of our questions to be answered. It is to know Him and experience His healing power. And as He heals and renews our hearts, the answers to all of our questions tend to matter much less.

Matilda had to walk through the process of forgiveness toward all those who had abused her and toward her father, who had neglected her and failed to protect her. She had to trust God to be her vindicator in those situations. She had to renew her mind to the truth that she was loved and that the phrase "once an addict, always an addict" did not have to be the reality in her life. She realized that her past did not have to determine her future.

I think that Matilda is a powerful example of someone who understands her authority as a daughter of God and how to stand in that authority! One of the most foundational pieces of our program at Mercy is helping our residents understand their authority in Christ. We believe that understanding what it means to stand in our authority is a game-changer when it comes to walking in freedom.

1 John 3:8 says that Jesus came to Earth to destroy the works of the enemy. And the cross is where Satan was defeated. When Jesus died on the cross, it *seemed* like Satan was victorious over Him. But on the third day, Jesus rose from the grave and therefore, triumphed over the enemy! In that moment, Satan was stripped of his authority.

In fact, before Jesus went back to heaven, he actually said in Matthew 28:18, "*All authority* in heaven and on earth has been given to me." And when we choose to commit our lives to Christ, we not only share in His death and His burial, but we also share in His resurrection, and therefore, His victory. Ephesians 2:6 says, "For he [God] raised us from the dead along with Christ and *seated us with him* in the heavenly realms because we are united with Christ Jesus." Christ is seated at the right hand of the Father—the seat of authority—and the Word says that we are actually seated with Him. When we are born again, we inherit the Name of Jesus, Whose Name is above every name, and now we have been given the right to *use* that Name against the enemy!

Your inheritance as a son or daughter of God is freedom. It's healing. It's forgiveness. It's love. It's joy. It's peace. And if you belong to Him, you get to claim those promises over your life. You get to claim your inheritance. Matilda received a revelation of her position as God's daughter while she was at Mercy, and it radically changed the way she approached every day and every difficulty.

Now, it's amazing to see how Matilda is comforting others with the same comfort that she has received (2 Corinthians 1:4). She and her husband are leaders in their St. Louis church, ministering to the hurting and broken within their own city. And I love how Matilda's journey has come full-circle with her now working at Mercy and encouraging young women who are in the same shoes she was in over five years ago. She is an incredible example of how mercy and freedom is multiplied through the young women who graduate from the Mercy program, and I could not be prouder of her!

reason

THIRTEEN

Brittany

Brittany was blessed with a beautiful smile that slowly became her mask. Born and raised in Rhode Island by hard-working Haitian immigrants, Brittany and her family—four kids, grandmother, uncle, mom and dad—lived in a one-bedroom apartment in a drug- and crime-plagued neighborhood. Sometimes the morning light revealed bodies shot and left on the sidewalk to die. When the family traveled, they snuck out in the middle of the night so nobody would rob their apartment.

Soon, her parents saved enough to buy a large house in the suburbs. The family, including cousins, uncles and aunts, moved in together. However, instead of welcoming them, kids in the predominantly white neighborhood terrorized them with racial epithets and hurled rocks.

"Immigrants don't belong here!" they shouted. "We're going to burn your house down."

Are they just taunting us, or do they really mean it? Brittany wondered. They targeted her especially because her skin was darker than the others'. Even in her community, darker skin was unwanted, and calling someone "dark" was an insult spoken in anger.

"You need to scrub your skin more when you shower," Brittany's mother advised. "You look like that because you don't scrub your skin enough."

Her parents worked most of the day and night, and when home, tempers often flared. Brittany and her three younger siblings were left in the care of their uncle who lived downstairs in the basement, and when harsh words came their way, he offered comfort.

"You're beautiful and I love you," he told Brittany after she was the subject of one of her mother's outbursts. "I wish I could take you to Haiti. The people there would call you beautiful."

But the relationship turned nightmarish when he began abusing her sexually. Brittany was five years old. Brittany learned to let her mind "disappear" and imagine herself in Haiti, wearing a beautiful dress, walking down sunshine streets with people telling her how pretty she was. Or she envisioned a relationship with her mom that did not exist, where her mom brushed Brittany's hair and made conversation and laughed easily.

Her uncle began controlling her routines and behaviors, becoming upset when Brittany didn't follow his rules. For example, she had to go downstairs to greet him first thing every morning, and as she got older, she was not allowed to show any interest in boys her age.

Most of all, she was not to tell anyone what he did to her.

"Don't say anything," was his mantra. "Keep this a secret between you and me."

At eight years old, Brittany began to wonder, *Why does my school teach us that kids are supposed to say no to strangers and certain physical touch? Why does my uncle want to keep what we do a secret? Why does it always happen at night? Why do I feel so bad when it happens? And if it's not bad, why can't I tell everyone else?*

Sensing her unease, her uncle shared the Bible story of Ruth and Boaz, using it as a supposed "example" of an older man loving a younger girl. He also began giving her a $20 bill each time he abused her. Money made Brittany popular at school, and kids stopped picking on her so much.

One day when she was 12, her father surprised her with a question: "Does anything inappropriate happen with your uncle?"

Fear lurched into her throat. Her uncle's admonitions were emblazoned on her mind.

"No," she replied to her father.

I don't want to betray my uncle, Brittany thought. *He really does love me. And it would harm our family. I have to keep everyone together.*

Her father looked at her a moment, trying to discern her level of honesty, then let the matter go.

One Saturday morning, when their family was hosting a church function at the house and many people were upstairs fellowshipping and eating, Brittany went down to the basement to greet her uncle. With him was a man from the church choir. Brittany loved singing in the choir and had been blessed with an angelic voice to accompany her beautiful smile. In worship, the presence of God felt so safe, warm and comforting. She never missed a Sunday morning. Now, the man from choir took her hand and pulled her onto his lap. She looked at her uncle to ask, *Is this okay?* His look told her it was. The man complimented her, stroked her hair, then let her go.

Shortly after that, he asked Brittany's parents if she could babysit while he and his wife were at work. But when Brittany came over, the man sexually abused her.

He is helping lead us in worship on Sundays and doing this to me in secret, Brittany thought. *This must be what God wants. That's why it's okay for him to do this.*

Shame twisted her church experience into something ugly. It was no longer a safe place, but a place of confusion and hypocrisy. Love, she concluded, was always sexual and predatory.

Anger rose behind her constant smile. At school, other students seemed so naive, so perfect, so protected. They were talking about kid shows on TV while Brittany was remembering the pornography her uncle had made her watch the night before. Even social relationships were not safe, because somehow her uncle found out if she talked to boys at school, and he berated her jealously.

Behind the mask, Brittany began to self-harm, and even contemplate suicide. For three years, the man from church abused her, supported by her uncle, who did as well.

Then, when Brittany was 18, her parents discovered that the same uncle was abusing her sister.

"That explains why you are constantly getting into trouble and fights at school!" her mother yelled angrily at her sister during a family meeting.

To Brittany, the news came as a betrayal. As awful as the relationship with her uncle was, she was emotionally tied to him and thought she was the sole recipient of his "affection." Brittany watched him swear on a Bible that he had not done what he was accused of doing to Brittany and her sister. His denial divided the family.

"Get your belongings and leave the house," Brittany's father told him. With no police involvement or counseling for the girls, 13 years of abuse ended in a moment.

With her uncle gone, Brittany's world turned upside down. Instead of relief, she felt chaos. His pervasive control had formed the architecture of her life—her schedule, her thoughts, her self-worth. Unable to function on her own, and with everyone else eager to leave the subject behind, Brittany was left with a heart full of anger, betrayal and wrong ideas about love. The stinging words of one relative hurt even worse: "You had a mouth to speak. You should have spoken up. You let this happen to you."

The only form of intimacy Brittany knew was sexual, and sexual involvement with a boy her age brought terrible flash-backs—and a pregnancy at 18 years old. Abortion followed, and then pills and then cutting to numb the pain. While driving to and from college in Connecticut, Brittany planned her last day: *I'm going to jump off this bridge,* she thought. *I have no reason to live.*

Before she could carry it through, a mental breakdown landed her in a psychiatric ward, and rumors spread through her church community that Brittany had had an abortion and was suicidal because of it. Many couldn't believe it.

"Not Brittany," they responded. "She's always smiling. She's so fun!"

Gripped by fear of making her family look bad, Brittany slipped into a catatonic state for three days. In her culture, "mental problems" were not given much legitimacy. Either you "had a spirit", or you were "crazy". But if emotions were troubling you, it was your job to be strong and get over them.

Her family visited the psych ward, but Brittany was barely aware of them. When they left, she had a terrifying dream. Seven figures—black silhouettes, shadows with no faces—came into her room and stood at the foot of her bed.

"We're here to get you," they announced.

The tall one in the middle had the silhouette of her uncle.

"We're here and it's time to go," they said.

"No, I'm not ready to go," Brittany objected.

"You have to go," they insisted, and became upset as the tall one—her uncle—jumped onto her bed and grabbed for her.

She woke up screaming, "I don't want to go!"

Her family's best advice remained, "You have to be stronger

than this. Show people what you are made of." So she pasted a big smile back on her face and continued participating in group therapy sessions with every appearance of optimism and confidence.

I've been fooling people my whole life, she thought. *This'll be easy.*

And it was. But back home, the church called her into a meeting to discipline her.

"We know you had an abortion," they said. "That's why you were hospitalized."

They're right, but that's not why I was hospitalized, she thought. *I could deny this, but why create lies to cover more lies? I'm tired of this foolishness.*

When they finished accusing her, Brittany said calmly, "I did have an abortion, but that's not why I was in the hospital. I tried to kill myself because I was sexually abused."

She gave them the entire story and showed them the cuts on her arms where she had harmed herself. Her parents appeared shocked and ashamed to have their dirty laundry aired. The pastors seemed taken aback that she was accusing a lay leader in the church. The youth pastor and his wife were crying and apologizing for pushing an inquiry without knowing all the facts.

Brittany became enraged with everyone.

"Now you're crying, when I've poured my guts out?" she shouted. "Where were you before, when everything seemed perfect?"

The choir member was called before the committee and denied everything. He even accused Brittany of initiating a relationship with him—at age 12. Undefended, disbelieved and betrayed, Brittany agreed to hurriedly marry the young man who had made her pregnant, but the marriage was quickly annulled, and Brittany moved to Florida, far away from most everyone she knew.

I shamed everyone in my family and community, she thought. *It's better if I just go. They don't want me around anyway.*

She soon found herself on the streets, trying to find food and shelter day by day. One day, a man pulled beside her in his car and struck up conversation.

Ah, she realized, *he thinks I'm one of the "girls."*

Brittany had discovered a culture of prostitution on the streets but avoided those parts of town. Now, presented with the possibility of a room somewhere—and money for her escalating drug habit— she thought to herself, *You're hungry. You haven't eaten in days. You have no money, nowhere to stay. What's one time? Make this money and you can get what you need.*

She got into the car. So began a vicious cycle of using drugs, prostitution, and looking for food and shelter. The money she made was never enough.

It's better than going back to Rhode Island, she thought at her worst moments, and at times her mind drifted to the place in her imagination where people called her beautiful.

Living in a drug-and-alcohol-induced haze, dark clouds seemed to gather around her. After a while she could barely tell the difference between being awake and asleep. Everything looked gray. A violent argument with the man she was living with, whom she barely knew, led to one last suicide attempt.

I know the end is near for me, she concluded. *I feel death right around me.*

The thought of dying seemed to give some comfort. But she ended up at the hospital, where not even Brittany's winning smile could convince them to let her go.

"You're not leaving without a long-term care plan," they insisted, seeming to sense that if they released her, she wouldn't live.

I can always talk my way out of these things, she fumed to herself. *God, I'm lost and broken. Just let me go—and let me die. Why am I still alive?*

I'm not finished with you yet, His voice said in her heart, faintly but surely. *I'm not letting you go.*

The name "Mercy Multiplied" came to mind, because a friend had recently sent Brittany a private message on social media to say, "Hey, this is really random but have you ever thought of going to Mercy?"

"That's not for me," Brittany had replied.

Now, stuck at a hospital, Mercy Multiplied seemed the best way out. Brittany started the application process and soon experienced a strange feeling: hope.

Then came one last dark dream. In it, Brittany was leaving on a trip, and people from all seasons of her life were coming to say good-bye—and mourn for her.

Everybody's wearing black and crying, Brittany thought. *Why so sad? I'm going away on a trip. Shouldn't they be happy?*

Still, they kept hugging her and saying good-bye as if it meant forever.

At the airport, a man with authority stopped her.

"You can't get on this flight," he said. "It's not yours. It's not time for you to go."

"It is time," Brittany replied, indicating her packed luggage. "Why can't I get on?"

"No, Brittany," he repeated, "it's not time for you to get on this flight."

She woke up confused. The possibility of death had never felt so close. And yet she believed that the dream told her it wasn't her time yet. The next day, she was accepted to the St. Louis Mercy Multiplied home.

Once there, her old thoughts and coping mechanisms returned with a vengeance.

When you go there, you show them you're a leader, she instructed herself. *You encourage those girls. Be strong!*

So Brittany bopped into the front door wearing a polka dot dress and a pretty necklace, smiling with every megawatt she could muster. Other girls thought she was a new staff member as she greeted everyone and exuded confidence.

Then came her first private counseling session.

"You don't have to wear that here," her counselor said.

"What are you talking about?" Brittany replied, smiling back.

"You can take off the mask while you're here," the counselor said.

"I don't have a mask," Brittany informed her.

"Okay, fine," the counselor said. "Whenever you want to take it off, go ahead. But you don't have to wear that here."

If I take off this mask and they see the damaged person I am, they'll kick me out of this program, Brittany admitted to herself. *They'll treat me the way everyone else treats me.*

In the days that followed, hearing from the other women in the program was a revelation.

They're just as broken as me, Brittany realized. *They walked in my shoes! I'm not some alien. It does happen to other people.*

The more they poured God's love into her, the more she opened the door to her heart, and for the first time had real conversations about her pain, trauma and betrayal. Little by little, the mask slipped off as Brittany encountered Jesus, realized her value and worth as God's child, and experienced a love that wasn't based on strength of personality or giving her body to be used. In counseling, she spoke hypothetically about her past or gave small amounts of information, just to see how her counselor reacted.

She keeps giving me love, no matter how much I open up, Brittany observed. *Is it possible I can really get this stuff out—all of it—and walk in the freedom they're talking about?*

Nightmares answered, "No."

She was talking about her uncle so much with the counselor that he began to appear in her dreams. One time, she became certain he was at the library at Mercy. Fear gripped her heart, and she began to doubt that coming to Mercy was the right choice. One morning, she packed her suitcases and told the staff, "I want to leave."

The home's program director came upstairs and sat on the bed with her.

"What is it, Brittany?" she asked.

"This is not for me," Brittany said firmly. "I'm going back."

"Why?"

"I just don't want to do this anymore. I . . . I don't think I'm capable of it," Brittany answered. The director nodded and waited for more.

"I had no idea how deep this would get," Brittany continued. "I thought it'd be a group of girls, we'd sing Kumbaya and I'd go home and say, 'I'm okay now, I went through the program.'"

"If you want to leave, we can't keep you here," the director said, "but when you walk out those doors, what will you do? Where are you going to go?"

There's nothing out there for you but death, Brittany told herself. And she broke down. Tears had never come like they did now. Every wall she had built to keep people from seeing her brokenness crumbled. Still, she heard old lies screaming for her attention:

Nobody can love you the way you love you! They're just going to send you to the psych ward like everybody else.

Your pain is yours! You're nobody without it.

Freedom is an illusion. What happened to you is real—own it. It is who you are.

But nobody shipped her off to a psych ward—in fact, they loved her all the more. Brittany let her real emotions come out, and instead of wearing a smile, sometimes in counseling she hung her head, or sat on the floor in the corner, fumbling her hands.

"Hey, you can lift your head," her counselor said. "You don't have to be ashamed."

She began to see God's hand in her life where she had not seen it before. Her own resilience and ability to survive was a gift from Him. As she prayed through past hurts, she felt God healing each one of them. After a while, true freedom took root. The smile returned—but it was real now. For the first time, she felt like her life was important and worthwhile. She felt true peace and saw a future for her life. The old identity of death and darkness was put into the past and the new Brittany began shining forth as who she really was. Graduation was a beautiful day.

While in the Mercy program, Brittany had attended a

women's conference at James River Church in Missouri. She had fallen in love with the church and felt the presence of God so powerfully there. So after graduating from Mercy, Brittany connected with James River Church again and ended up working there for a year. She lived with a wonderful family who opened their home, and she established consistent, healthy life habits she had learned at Mercy. Day by day, she walked in freedom from past hurts and habits.

After spending a year in Missouri, Brittany enrolled at Northpoint Bible College and began attending in the fall of 2014. On a mission trip to the Netherlands with her school, the group leader gently invited her to share her testimony. Brittany wasn't sure.

Is this the right time? she prayed.

She was always careful how and where she shared her story, because of the nature of what had happened, and to protect her own heart. Now she was in a foreign country, in a culture she didn't understand, with people she didn't know.

I don't know, Lord, she prayed. *I'm not sure I should.*

A familiar voice reminded her, *You said you would share your testimony if I gave you the opportunity. I'm giving you this opportunity.*

So Brittany stepped bravely forward when invited by the pastor, and by the time she was finished, nearly everyone from the sound board to the front row was in tears—not tears of heaviness but of freedom. Brittany knew the Holy Spirit was working through her words to lead others out of prisons of shame.

After the service, a fragile, gray-haired lady approached. Brittany could sense her strong faith, but the lines and wrinkles on her face told a story of heartache as well.

"I am 85 years old," the woman said, then hesitated before continuing: "I was abused as a child. This morning I was crying before coming here because of the pain of my past, and so I asked God for a sign. Then I heard your testimony, and I understood that my past doesn't have to define me."

She gripped Brittany's hand tightly.

"We overcome by the blood of the Lamb and word of our testimony," she said, eyes glistening with newfound hope and assurance.

Brittany graduated from Northpoint Bible College in May of 2018 with a double major—one in Biblical Studies and the other in Worship Arts. She eventually wants to get her Masters degree in Human Service Counseling with a focus in Crisis Intervention.

Brittany currently works with a sex and domestic violence agency serving public schools, and became Rhode Island's first school-based advocate for student victims—the kind of advocate she didn't have as a child. She is working on creating an expressive arts program for the agency, so that the students can have a place to express their emotions in a positive way.

One day, Brittany went to her childhood middle school to meet with the principal and caught sight of her face in a graduation picture.

Look at me back then, Brittany thought. *Broken, depressed, seeing no hope for the future. I remember hiding in the bathroom for hours in this very building because I didn't know how I would get through the day.*

Tears streamed down her cheeks.

What a blessing and a miracle to be alive today, she thought. *God has been good! He does save and is gracious. I'm so proud of where I am now, helping girls like me who didn't have this kind of program before. Mercy planted that seed in me—this is the fruit of Mercy. Thank you, Jesus!*

_____

It makes me sick to my stomach knowing that Brittany was not only abused by a family member, but also by a leader within her church. Sadly, stories of sexual abuse within church walls are running rampant today. I can only imagine how heartbroken God must be when His own people, and leaders within His church, are the perpetrators of such horrible things.

Over my years of leading Mercy Multiplied, I have become extremely passionate about the importance of people in leadership – whether it be in churches, corporations, non-profits or ministries – being willing to get help when they need help. It is common for men and women in leadership roles to think that they must "have it all together." They fear that if people know they are struggling, they could risk losing their positions, or at least the respect of all those who follow them.

I understand this struggle, because in 2001 when my dad passed away, all kinds of pain and heartache from my childhood rose to the surface. I knew the Holy Spirit had allowed these things to rise up, because it was His timing for me to deal with them. As the founder of a ministry that I had been leading for 17 years, I was stunned when these issues rose to the surface because I thought that I had already dealt with them.

I had a decision to make: I could forge ahead in pride and try to hide the issues, or I could humbly seek out the help that

I knew I needed. At the urging of a close personal friend, I made the choice to go to a licensed Christian counselor. This was the beginning of seven years of counseling and healing that significantly impacted my life, and it was one of the best decisions I ever made. (You can read more about my journey in my book, *Mission of Mercy*.) Seeking out the help that I needed not only changed my life, but it also changed the entire culture of Mercy. When I became open and transparent with my team, they became much more open and transparent with me. I am convinced that I probably wouldn't still be leading Mercy today if I hadn't been willing to deal with the stuff God brought to the surface at that time.

No leader is perfect. We all have areas of pain and struggle in our lives that the Lord wants to work on so that we can walk in greater freedom today than we did yesterday. Remember that you can only take others as far as you have come, so it is important that you are working through your own areas of struggle as the Lord leads you to do so. Seek out godly counsel and wisdom and work through those things when they arise. Like me, you may choose to get a counselor or pastoral support as well. There is no shame in getting help, only celebration!

The bottom line is this: you give away what you carry. If you carry brokenness and bondage, that is what you will ultimately give away. But if you carry life and freedom, that is what you will give away. Many people have heard the phrase, "Hurt people, hurt people." At Mercy, we believe that the opposite is true too and often say, "Free people, free people!"

Your willingness to seek healing and freedom in your own life will greatly enhance your leadership. However, if you choose to ignore your issues, they will undoubtedly affect your leadership, and you may end up hurting others in the process.

As I often say, "If you don't deal with your issues, your issues will deal with you!" That's exactly what happened in Brittany's story. A leader in the Church, who was clearly living in his own struggles and bondage, ended up being one of her primary abusers. Church was no longer a safe place for Brittany. It's heartbreaking, and it is all too common of an issue.

Before coming to Mercy, Brittany epitomized the countless people who are hurting and struggling but choose to cover their issues with a fake smile and false strength. Her culture told her that she simply needed to "get over" her issues, that she just needed to be strong. And while this was a defining characteristic of her family's culture, this way of thinking has infiltrated innumerable cultures. Strength and resiliency are prized, while struggle and weakness are looked down upon.

I'm sure we can all look back and recognize times in our lives when we were hurting and struggling, and instead of being honest with trusted people in our lives, we plastered on our fake smiles and acted like we had everything together. I'm sure, if we were honest, we would all admit that those attempts to "fix" ourselves or simply act like everything was okay never brought true freedom; in fact, they typically just leave us feeling frustrated and alone.

My friend, it's okay to not be okay; it's just not okay to stay there! Scripture is very clear that you are not alone in your struggles. Romans 3:23 says that *all* have sinned and fallen short. 1 John 1:10 says that if we say that we aren't guilty of sin, we actually make God out to be a liar and His word isn't in us. Proverbs 28:14 says that anyone who tries to hide his sins will not prosper, but the person who confesses their sins and chooses to leave them behind will find mercy.

Thankfully, Scripture also reminds us that God is compassionate, merciful, slow to get angry and filled with unfailing love (Psalm 103:8). We don't have to put on our fake smiles in front of Him. He is intimately aware of our every thought, every word, and every action. And while that truth can terrify some people, it is one of the most freeing realities that you can experience when you understand that our God of grace knows everything there is to know about you, yet still welcomes you into His arms every moment of every day. Romans 8 reminds us that there is no condemnation for those who are in Christ. His heart towards you doesn't change one bit, whether you're living your best day or your worst.

At Mercy, Brittany not only learned how to take off her mask with God, she also learned how to take it off with others who she trusted. She experienced God's grace and acceptance through the Mercy staff, and it wasn't until she was willing to open her heart, to be honest and real, to be seen and fully known, that she was able to find true healing and freedom.

Brittany's story of transformation is truly miraculous. Her life was weighed down with darkness and death when she arrived at Mercy, but today, she is the epitome of life and *true*, authentic joy, not the fake kind that she had worn in the past. Her testimony has impacted many people, and I particularly love the story of the 85-year-old woman who came up to Brittany after she spoke on her mission trip, and the woman shared about what God was teaching her in regard to her own childhood abuse. It just goes to show that we are all a work in progress. You are never too old to discover new levels of healing and freedom in your life. God always has more, and we are all on this journey together!

Conclusion

I have shared with you 13 stories of how God brought radical healing and freedom into seemingly hopeless situations, and I could tell you countless more about men and women outside the walls of Mercy who have experienced life transformation through the same principles of freedom that we teach in our residential program. Freedom is not just available to those who are residents in one of our Mercy homes. It's available to *you* as well. God can, and will, move powerfully if you choose to allow Him to work in your heart and life.

Every day, testimonies pour in to our Outreach team about how God is using what was developed at Mercy Multiplied to bring freedom and life to every corner of the earth. Testimonies like the one we received from a man in Tennessee named Jason, who had dealt with a sense of overwhelming bitterness and anger throughout much of his life. When Jason got married and he and his wife had a son, he had a deep desire to be emotionally stable for his family. But in times of stress and disappointment, it felt almost impossible to control his emotions. He shared with us, "When I most wanted to be a comfort to my family, I instead gave in to an overwhelming feeling of anger. My anger and bitterness was destructive to my family and a source of great shame for me."

Jason was given a copy of Mercy's *Keys to Freedom*, and as he worked through the study, he realized that his anger had a root cause, and if he would let God remove the root, he could have victory over his emotions. While praying through the principles in the study, Jason identified that the root cause of his bitterness and anger was unforgiveness, and he needed to forgive his parents for some trauma from his past. Jason shared, "Working through the study was not easy, but after making the choice to forgive my parents, there was a noticeable change in my behavior. I felt more at peace with myself. I no longer felt out of control. More importantly, I have seen a change in my family. My relationship with my son has changed. He is at ease around me, and I am finally proud of myself."

Or there's the testimony that we received from Jane, a woman from Uganda whose life was radically transformed by the principles of freedom in my book, *Ditch the Baggage*. Jane shared that she was helpless and filled with bitterness until her pastor in Uganda gave her the book. Through *Ditch the Baggage*, Jesus healed Jane from years of pain and suffering caused by a traumatic rape and unplanned pregnancy. Jane told us, "It has really changed my life. The principles of freedom in this book have taught me to love, to forgive, and to heal." Now, equipped with *Keys to Freedom*, Jane continues to lead other hurting Ugandan women to Jesus so that they can experience the same freedom and life transformation.

I am so excited about how God is using the principles of freedom that are being shared through Mercy's Outreach Program to impact the lives of men and women of all ages! However, if you are a young woman between the ages of 13–28 and are hurting or struggling, you can get information about Mercy's residential program and apply to the program at www.MercyMultiplied.com. I encourage you to not wait one more day to take a step toward the freedom that Jesus Christ has available for you! I can assure you that if you walk through the doors of one of our Mercy homes, you will be welcomed with open arms. If you open your heart to God, your life will be changed forever. He is with you and will meet you right where you are.

If you *know* a young woman between the ages of 13–28 who needs help, please consider sharing the testimonies of transformation from this book with her and let her know about Mercy's residential program. Remind her that there is hope and encourage her to consider applying to the program, or perhaps simply coming and taking a tour of one of the Mercy homes.

Lastly, if this book has inspired you to help others find freedom in Christ and you would like to consider donating to Mercy Multiplied, you can do so at www.MercyMultiplied. com/Donate.

No matter who you are or what you have done, the same radical life transformation that you have read about in the pages of this book is possible for you and for those you love. Through the power of Christ, you can overcome whatever issues or hurts you may be struggling with. There is true healing and lasting freedom available to you!

Prayer of Salvation

God loves you—no matter who you are, no matter what your past. God loves you so much that He gave His one and only begotten Son for you. The Bible tells us that ". . . whoever believes in him shall not perish but have eternal life" (John 3:16 NIV). Jesus laid down His life and rose again so that we could spend eternity with Him in heaven and experience His absolute best on earth. If you would like to receive Jesus into your life, say the following prayer out loud and mean it from your heart.

Heavenly Father, I come to You admitting that I am a sinner. Right now, I choose to turn away from sin, and I ask You to cleanse me of all unrighteousness. I believe that Your Son, Jesus, died on the cross to take away my sins. I also believe that He rose again from the dead so that I might be forgiven of my sins and made righteous through faith in Him. I call upon the name of Jesus Christ to be the Savior and Lord of my life. Jesus, I choose to follow You and ask that You fill me with the power of the Holy Spirit. I declare that right now I am a child of God. I am free from sin and full of the righteousness of God. I am saved in Jesus' name. Amen.

NEED HELP?

If you're a young woman between

the ages of 13–28

CALL OR APPLY TODAY!

615.831.6987 or visit
MercyMultiplied.com

There is no problem too big
or too small for God.

Below are a few life-controlling issues the young women
who come to Mercy Multiplied face:

DEPRESSION · SELF-HARM · EATING DISORDERS

ADDICTION · UNPLANNED PREGNANCY

ABUSE · SEX TRAFFICKING

Mercy Multiplied is a **free of charge** Christian residential program
and we want to help!

He heals the brokenhearted and binds up their wounds
Psalm 147:3

FREEDOM
Series

If you want to learn more about how to apply the principles of freedom discussed in this book to your own life, check out our *Freedom Series*.

Mercy Multiplied's Freedom Series is for anyone wanting to live free and stay free. This life-changing series teaches a biblical model for freedom and offers the 7 practical keys that have proven transformational to thousands of hurting young women in Mercy's residential program for over three decades. Each resource—a book and videos by Nancy Alcorn and an in-depth study for personal or group use—is a valuable tool to discover the keys to healing and freedom in Jesus Christ! Choose 1 or all 3 to walk in greater freedom!

For more information, visit MercyMultiplied.com/FreedomSeries

Helpful Resources
Free e-books available online at MercyMultiplied.com/FreeBooks

Mercy For **Series**

This incredible four-book series covers the topics of eating disorders, self-harm, addictions and sexual abuse. These books are written to help bring freedom to all who are struggling with these issues. However, these books are also designed for family members, friends, youth leaders, senior pastors—all those who care about someone who is struggling with these issues or who desires to help someone who is struggling with these issues. (Also available in print. Spanish versions available as free e-books only.)

Beyond **Series**

The Beyond Series presents personal stories from girls who have found freedom from self-harm and eating disorders and guides readers through practical steps to break free from these self-destructive behaviors. (Also available in print. Spanish versions available as free e-books only.)

"Mercy For" and "The Beyond Series: Real Stories of Freedom" are not designed to be a replacement for professional help; it is recommended that girls struggling with self-harm or an eating disorder use these books in conjunction with Christian counseling or mentoring.

To learn more about how the principles of freedom have impacted Mercy Multiplied Founder and President, Nancy Alcorn, check out her book *Mission of Mercy*.

"There is nothing closer
to the heart of God than to help
heal the brokenhearted. This
is the driving force behind the
work of Nancy Alcorn."

—JOEL OSTEEN

Mission of
MERCY

Allowing God to Use YOU to Make a Difference in Others

- Are you willing to be part of the answer?
- Can God trust you to love the unlovable?
- Will you move past judgment to compassion?

NANCY ALCORN
FOUNDER AND PRESIDENT OF MERCY MINISTRIES

Mission of Mercy

In "Mission of Mercy," Nancy Alcorn challenges readers to consider why people behave the way they do, sharing the practical principles that have made Mercy Multiplied such a success at life transformation. Illustrated by the touching, inspiring testimonies of real women — including gripping portions of Nancy's own story that have never before been published — she demonstrates how each of us can move from a place of judgment to compassion that leads to action.

Outreach

Equipping Churches. Educating Leaders. Empowering Individuals.

Listen to our Podcast!

Free weekly podcast where we discuss real-life issues applying biblically based principles of freedom. Available on iTunes or MercyTalk.org

MPower Workshops

Do you have a heart for helping people who are hurting and struggling? MPower Workshops can help you understand more about how to help and support others, while staying healthy and whole in the process.

Freedom Advocacy Program

Our Freedom Advocacy Program equips men and women to effectively empower those who are struggling in a way that brings about true healing and life transformation within their communities, churches, schools, and more.

For more information visit MercyMultiplied.com/Outreach

SPONSOR A *girl*

—LIKE SOPHIE—

Today...

I KNOW WHO I AM IN CHRIST.

I KNOW MY PURPOSE IN LIFE.

I AM A NEW CREATION.

I AM **FREE.**

When you sponsor a girl at Mercy Multiplied, you help provide valuable financial support for her room and board, counseling, life-skills training and spiritual growth. Most importantly, you make an eternal difference in her sense of self-worth. Will you help a girl who feels worthless realize the priceless treasure she is in the eyes of God?

MercyMultiplied.com/SponsorAGirl

Become a Monthly Partner for **less than $1 a day**
and watch a life be transformed!

Our Team Mercy 360 Members receive:

A free customizable t-shirt to wear proudly in the style
and color of your choice.

A free annual entry into one of our "Run For Mercy 5K
and Family Walk" events.

An exclusive opportunity to send hope-filled messages
to the Mercy residents.

Sign up today at TeamMercy360.com

Get Involved with

You can play a key role in Mercy Multiplied's ongoing work to restore the lives of young women in need and help all people live in freedom!! There are many ways to help. Join us today!

 ## ATTEND

our Benefits, Luncheons, 5K Races, Nancy Alcorn's Speaking Engagements

 ## GIVE

to Team Mercy 360, Sponsor A Girl, Planned Giving

 ## PRAY

for Applicants, Residents, Graduates, Mercy Staff

 ## VOLUNTEER

at Mercy Events, Homes or Corporate Headquarters, Internships

For more information, please visit
MercyMultiplied.com

For more information on Mercy and its global affiliates please visit **MercyMultiplied.com**.

For constant updates, follow us on social media!

FIND US ON FACEBOOK:
Facebook.com/MercyMultiplied
Facebook.com/NancyAlcorn

FIND US ON INSTAGRAM:
Instagram.com/MercyMultiplied
Instagram.com/NancyAlcorn

FIND US ON TWITTER:
Twitter.com/MercyMultiplied
Twitter.com/NancyAlcorn